D1333076

BIRDWATCHING with Bill Oddie

BIRDWATCHING with Bill Oddie

MACMILLAN

To the late David Hunt
Great birdwatcher ... great friend

Published 1988 by
THE MACMILLAN PRESS LTD
London and Basingstoke

Associated companies in Auckland, Delhi, Dublin, Gabarone, Hamburg,
Harare, Hong Kong, Johannesburg, Kuala Lumpur, Lagos, Manzini,
Melbourne, Mexico City, Nairobi, New York, Singapore, Tokyo

British Library Cataloguing in Publication Data

Oddie, Bill
    Birdwatching with Bill Oddie.
    1. Bird watching—Europe
    I. Title
    598'.07'2344   QL690.A1

    ISBN 0-333-46668-3

Designed by Robert Updegraff
Typeset by Florencetype Ltd, Kewstoke, Avon
Printed by Unwin Brothers Limited,
The Gresham Press, Old Woking, Surrey GU22 9LH

Contents

Foreword

Birdwatching. You can do it anywhere. From inside your home, out in your garden, on your way to work or school, in the town or in the country, at weekends or on holiday, in Britain or abroad. It's a hobby for anywhere and everywhere and for everyone and anyone.

Some people are quite happy feeding the ducks in the park or putting out peanuts and crumbs – to them 'birds' probably means mainly tits, thrushes, robins and blackbirds . . . garden birds. Others prefer getting away for a day to a local reservoir, or even a bird reserve, discovering a whole bewildering new range of species: terns, waders, wildfowl. Or you can go twitching: chasing after rare birds.

There are serious ornithologists with specialist interests: helping to protect rare breeding birds, or studying a particular species or group of birds; sea-bird specialists, or wildfowl specialists; birds of prey experts; studying migration routes or trapping, ringing, weighing and measuring birds, constantly analysing. There are bird photographers and there are bird artists. And indeed there are people who write bird books!

All in their different ways, birdwatchers. Which are you? It's up to you. I have met beginners who are intimidated by 'experts' and experts who are scornful of beginners. They've *all* got it wrong. The great thing about birdwatching is that it can be enjoyed on so many levels – and it doesn't matter what level you choose, it's equally fascinating, equally enjoyable.

However, whether you are a beginner or an expert, a garden bird spotter, a heavy 'twitcher' or a serious ornithologist, you'll want to know *what* you're looking at: the names of birds, which is which and why. It's true there's a lot more to a total study of ornithology than identification, but bird recognition is surely the basis for all other interests. The kind of questions I'm frequently asked confirm this. Broadly they fall into two categories – 'Please can you tell me what I need to start seeing birds?' and 'Please can you tell me the name of something I've already seen?'.

So, in this book I'm going to attempt to answer those questions. I feel pretty confident about the first one. The second question, however, is a bit trickier. In fact, I can't promise to answer it at all . . . but I hope I *can* help you find out the answer for yourself.

Bill Oddie

Essential Equipment

Before I go out for a day's birdwatching I have a little checklist I tick off as I leave the house: 'Binoculars . . . telescope . . . notebook . . . pencil'. Other things can help the day along – like food, maps, money and so on – but the essential gear without which I simply couldn't enjoy the day is: 'Binoculars . . . telescope . . . notebook . . . pencil'. These are the things I really must never forget.

Strictly speaking, I suppose I shouldn't forget clothes either but I find that I rarely do! Mind you, odds and ends like gloves, woolly hat and so on *are* easy enough to leave behind. So, come to think of it maybe we should start with. . . .

Birdwatching Clothes

You want to see birds but you don't want birds to see you. I know this may seem pretty obvious but it's amazing how many birdwatchers take to the field looking positively luminous, wearing orange and yellow anoraks that would be more appropriate on a motorway maintenance team. Not only do these act as brilliant bird-scaring jackets even at considerable distances, they also rustle when you move and are as upsetting to birds in a wood as sweet papers are to people in a cinema. So as a general rule: keep it soft and dull. Browns, greens, greys, ochres and the like. The exception to this rule is when you are abroad in countries where birdwatchers' paramilitary ex-army gear is all too easily mistaken for terrorists' 'uniform', especially if you are stalking stealthily through the jungle or lurking on the fringe of a 'sensitive' area. This really *is* a serious warning. Over the past few years quite a few birders have been shot at or arrested for spying. So when birding abroad wear your holiday shirts and shorts and *look* like a foreigner – the white legs may well help too! However, back to Britain, where happily it's much safer. . . .

Apart from this general rule – soft and dull – it's more or less up to you what you wear. However, bear in mind the vagaries of the English weather. Unfortunately as we all know within the same day it can easily be wet and dry, hot and cold. The secret has to be layers. If you set off in a huge thick arran sweater and a heavily lined oiled jacket you haven't got many choices if the sun comes out. You can boil or strip. A more versatile ensemble would be a thermal vest, a t-shirt, a sweatshirt and a lightweight waterproof. It will probably be just as warm but if it gets *too* hot it's no great embarrassment to nip behind a bush and peel off a layer, which can then be stuffed in the anorak pocket or rolled up and tied around your waist.

There are two items you may be tempted to spend extra money on. The first is a pair of boots or wellies. I have to confess *my* feet are a problem. All my life I've conducted a never-ending quest to find a *really* comfortable pair of walking boots. As a teenager I never found anything that didn't need at least a month breaking in, during which time I was often reduced to a near cripple by blisters. I remember this happening to me on, of all places, Fair Isle – a birdwatcher's Mecca – where I spent several days literally crawling after various rarities. In desperation I then switched to wellies which was when I discovered that if you intend to walk for six hours up and down hills in pursuit of a Little Bunting, wellies are not ideal footwear either.

You *will* need a pair of wellies. They are essential if you know you're going to be wading in water or slurping through soft mud. They're also pretty cosy if you're sitting for a long time in one place – say, in a hide or watching the sea – but they are *not* good for long long walks. Having said that, I admit for years I found them preferable to boots, especially if I turned the tops down to let a bit more air to my calves.

Eventually though boot manufacturers became more sympathetic to my tender tootsies and sometime back in the seventies I discovered what I think were then called 'nature boots' or something. They were made of very soft leather indeed, had no hard instep or heel and were moulded in a gentle rounded shape that looked like a paw but was bliss to walk in. Their only flaw was they weren't entirely waterproof – although I improved this with a special spray. They were also *so* soft that after a year or two they disintegrated. They weren't cheap either. Nevertheless, they were so comfortable I happily went back for another pair, only to discover the shop had closed down and the manufacturers had gone bankrupt.

So for a few more years it was back to wellies and a limp. For everyday wear (not birdwatching that is) I've always favoured track shoes or trainers – which is probably why my feet have never got on well with big hard boots. For much of my life this has made me a bit of a social outcast; by and large grey suits and smart ties don't go very well with trainers, so I never have managed to look 'respectable'.

Happily though, foot fashions have changed and nowadays of course *everyone*'s wearing trainers and, better news still, many boot manu-facturers have produced a splendid sort of hybrid that looks like and is as snug as a track shoe yet is *almost* as sturdy as a walking boot. So *that*'s the one for me.

But enough of my feet (as indeed I've often said myself). With any luck *you* don't have such problems. Anyway, a quick recap of the choices.

- Walking boots: great if you can wear them; waterproof if possible.
- Wellies: essential for wet places but not recommended for hiking.
- And for softies like me – trainer style boots, or even track shoes and risk getting wet feet!

Actually here's a good tip: it's the soggy socks that are *really* squelchy, so always keep a dry pair handy.

Now, the second potentially expensive item. The waterproof jacket . . . anorak . . . windcheater . . . protective clothing – call it what you will. There are a lot advertised. Some of them are *very* expensive, well over

£100, and even the cheapest are liable to be £30 or £40. Before I risk discussing them a little I'd like to make a general statement about value for money when buying birdwatching equipment. The same principle applies to jackets, binoculars, telescopes or books.

There's lots of good stuff on the market. There's also lots of pretty bad stuff (or should I say 'not so good'?) It all costs money. The good stuff isn't necessarily more expensive and even if it is it's often well worth paying that little bit extra. It's certainly as easy to buy the good stuff as the bad and it truly upsets me when I see people who've bought, as it were, the *wrong* things. It's by no means always their fault . . . advertising can be very persuasive, 'special offers' can be almost irresistible, and, worst of all, some shops have business deals with suppliers, publishers and so on that means that they simply don't stock some of the better items, whilst pushing less good products.

So when I'm dealing with the various essential items of birdwatching gear there's likely to be as many 'don'ts' as 'dos'. In other words, I'm going to try to warn you what *not* to buy and how to get the best value for money. What you ultimately *do* buy will probably be down to your personal taste – but whatever it is, we'll try and make sure it's the good stuff.

So . . . back to those weatherproof jackets. First decision: how weatherproof do you want it? To keep out showers? Or torrential rain? All the best makes have a little label or card attached telling you just how waterproof the material is. Some of them admit 'Showerproof – not totally rainproof. Whilst others claim, and I quote, to present 'an almost totally impervious barrier to wind and water'. This is the 'blurb' attached to some garments made from a certain pretty well-respected fabric that I won't name because it doesn't seem fair to single out one 'sinner' when there may be more. Nevertheless, here comes a cautionary tale!

I recently visited an outdoor clothing specialist and tried on a smock-type anorak that I liked immediately. The shop assistant assured me that it was genuinely waterproof and so I bought it. I found the material lightweight, comfy and a delight to wear – until I got caught in the rain. It wasn't even heavy rain, but in a very short time damp patches were seeping through to my sweatshirt in several places. I returned the jacket to the manufacturers who were very polite and equally apologetic. They explained that this particular material, *double* strength, is *almost* waterproof (but not quite!) but that *single* strength could hardly be described as more than 'showerproof'. 'If that!' I suggested. *My* smock was of course single strength. They offered to replace it with a double strength version, but I didn't want that because it lacked the lightness of the one I'd bought. I was definitely disappointed. I quoted the card: '. . . an almost totally impervious barrier to wind and water.' (It didn't mention anything about 'single or double'). Then I noticed that the paragraph ended: 'An additional proofing keeps the garment shower-proof in light rain.' Eh?! Now is that or is that not a contradiction in terms? What on earth is a 'showerproof impervious barrier'? I mean is it waterproof or isn't it? Clearly, in this case the answer was 'No, it isn't'. Comfy, warm, windproof, yes, but waterproof no.

Actually, I still wear the smock, but I now keep a light 'plastic' cagoul stuffed in the pocket! I do feel though that I must urge prospective buyers to rigorously question the weather-proofing claims of your intended purchase, and also make sure you can take the garment back if it proves to be less efficient than you were led to believe.

Anyway, for the moment, unless you too fancy the 'pac-a-mac in the pocket' technique, I shall assume that most birdwatchers prefer some-thing totally rainproof. So, that's one decision made. It means you're probably into the fairly expensive league already. Fortunately I think it really is true to say that all the top-grade manufacturers are pretty good and there's really not a bewilderingly huge choice anyway, so *whatever* you get it's likely to be OK. What you *do* have to decide is what kind of material you prefer. Truly weatherproof coats are either 'waxed' – so the texture is slightly oily, which some people don't like – or very very finely woven 'Goretex' type material which does have a pleasanter feel but certainly isn't cheap.

The other choice is lightweight or heavyweight? Or unlined or lined? The heavy, lined jackets are extremely snug but you'd get very hot in one if the day warmed up. Lighter ones perhaps lend themselves better to the 'layers' method of dressing as they can be easily discarded, rolled up and tied round your waist like a belt.

The other thing to check is the number and size of pockets. Remember you may want to carry note books, field guide, lens cloths, sandwiches, Mars bars, car keys and so on. Also, do you want a hood attached or do you prefer wearing a hat?

Whatever you go for, do buy from a specialist dealer who stocks a good range. If possible go along and try on a few and don't be misled by the sales assistant. Or you may do your research first – ask other bird-watchers what they recommend, and buy mail order from one of the stockists who advertise in specialist magazines. Whilst I think of it, this isn't a bad rule for when you're thinking of buying *any* birding gear – get the RSPB's magazine *Birds*, or *British Birds*, or *Bird Watching* magazine or *BBC Wildlife Magazine* and have a look at the adverts which will give you a list of current ranges and prices. (See Magazines, page 188.)

To help you make a final choice there's a list of 'favourite jackets' on page 194 as worn and recommended by readers of *British Birds*.

A final word on bits and pieces.

Gloves – so easy to forget but well worth remembering to slip into your pocket especially if you're going to be fairly static on a cold day, maybe scanning across a reservoir or sea-watching. They can restrict your dexterity with binoculars, telescope, or notebook and pencil – so make sure they're not too clumsy. I find the cheap 'fingerless' type are often a good compromise.

Hats – your chance for a bit of individuality. Anything goes really – I've seen birdwatchers sporting everything from toppers to sombreros, though woolly 'tea-cosies' seem to be most popular. They are usually festooned with bird-club badges which I'd like to think impresses the birds and makes them more willing to be watched.

Binoculars

There is no sadder person than a birdwatcher who's forgotten his or her binoculars! 'Bins' are to a birdwatcher as an instrument is to a musician, or a racket to a tennis player. Whenever I go abroad the only things I *really* worry about are my passport and my binoculars. They are always in my hand luggage. Usually in my hands.

Actually, I can think of *one* sadder person – that's the birdwatcher whose binoculars have broken. He'll be sad – and indeed angry – if for no other reason than that he's just realized he bought the wrong pair. It needn't ever happen. There are quite a few absolutely brilliant binoculars available; there are also lots and lots of very good ones; and there are

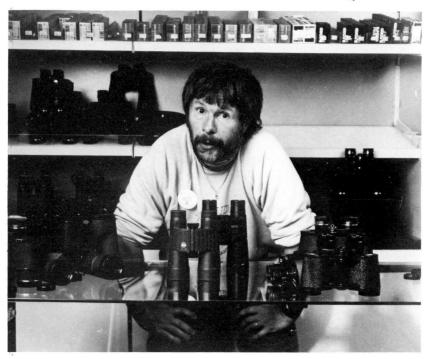

plenty of perfectly adequate ones. There is also a dangerous number of lousy ones. So first, let's avoid those. Let's be positive though and start with a do. *Do* go to a specialist dealer who stocks a wide selection of different makes. Refer to those magazine adverts again. There are several companies who have showrooms where you'll get expert advice and be allowed to take as long as you like. Some of them are even specially located with a view from the window that will allow you to test the equipment on real birds! So, if at all possible, go along in person and try a wide range. You'll also find that prices of binoculars vary from dealer to dealer and these specialists will usually give you the best discount. There *are* shops in cities and towns which have a fair range of binoculars but I have to advise that I don't think the high street camera shop is usually the best place to buy. The selection tends to be small, the prices high, and the testing conditions inadequate.

If you can't get along to a good showroom you may decide to mail order but first do your research. Find out what other birdwatchers use and ask them if you can have a quick glance through their binoculars –

but make sure you don't do it just as a rare bird flies past! The good mail order firms will then allow you to have binoculars on a week or two's approval so you can't really lose.

One big don't. Please *don't* buy the sort of binoculars often advertised in the Saturday morning papers. You know what I mean: 'Zungel & Phumph Ex-Army Binoculars. Giveaway prices. Magnifying 15 or 20 times. Ideal for birdwatching.' No, they're not. They're lousy for birdwatching. Why? Because they are invariably big and clumsy, the picture too dark, and the field of view too narrow, and in fact they magnify *too* much. I'll explain what I mean.

On any pair of binoculars there are two numbers. It'll say something like 8 × 30 or 10 × 40 or even 15 × 40. The first number is how many times they magnify. So, yes, a bird is brought 15 or 20 times closer and fills the view as it were. This is fine if it doesn't move, but if it does – and birds do tend to – it's extremely difficult to follow it. Moreover a 15 × binocular is likely to be so heavy that you'll find it very hard to hold them steady, and if you hang them round your neck you'll be left with a permanent stoop – you probably won't see many birds unless they perch on your feet!

So . . . the ideal magnification for birdwatching is between 7 and 10. You'll find that very few binoculars are sold that aren't within this range.

The second number refers to the diameter of the objective lens (the big one) in millimetres and, therefore, the bigger it is, the greater is the light

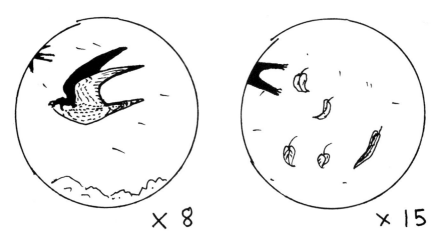

Following a flying bird is almost impossible at high magnification.

gathering power of the binoculars. The higher the number the more light is let in and the brighter the image. The more the binoculars magnify, however, the more light you need. So a pair of 10 × 40s would give a good bright picture but a pair of 15 × 40s would look pretty murky especially in gloomy weather. Second simple rule – if you divide the second number by the first it should come to about 4. You'll find that is the case with most of the popular binoculars . . . they'll be 8 × 30, or 9 × 35 or 10 × 40 or thereabouts. You *can* also get 7 × 50 (and 7 into 50 is over 7!) which will give a very bright image, that will almost illuminate the scene at dawn or dusk, but they tend to be for more specialist needs like, for example, owl or bat-watching.

Just as binoculars can be too big, they can also be too small. Some of them look like high-class opera glasses. They are tiny and can literally be slipped into a pocket, and I can well understand how people are tempted to buy them – they seem *so* convenient. However, I really *don't* recommend them. They are usually 8 × 20 or 10 × 25 which means the light gathering is poor but worse still, although the field of view is theoretically quite wide, the small lenses give a very restricted feeling to the picture that seems to cause real problems.

I once went to the Norfolk Broads on a testing day for binoculars where a group of beginners were able to try out a whole range. Many people were attracted to using the mini binoculars until, after half an hour, they began to wonder why some of us seemed to be seeing far more birds than they. Time and again I'd point out a flying bird that they simply couldn't pick up quickly enough. Once they swapped to the 8 × 30s or 10 × 40s they did much better.

So let's assume that's the sort of thing you're going to consider buying. How much should you pay? Well, you *can* pay in the region of £500 and you'll certainly get a superb pair of binoculars, but don't worry, you can also pay a great deal less and be perfectly satisfied. I suppose if I had to put a figure on it at time of writing I'd say roughly between £100 and £250 would give you a very wide choice of some excellent equipment. In fact I'm pretty sure you could look through some £500 pairs and then some £100 and not actually *see* much difference.

So what are you paying the extra for?

Well – apart from a possible tinge of snob-appeal – reliability, consistency and durability. Your £400 or £500 pair really can and should last you a lifetime and they'll put up with all sorts of harsh conditions. Theoretically you should be able to drop them onto rocks or dangle them in the sea and they'll survive unharmed (although I don't actually suggest you try it). They should let in neither dust nor moisture, and the optical performance should be impeccable.

I keep saying 'should' because even Rolls Royces break down so I guess the poshest binoculars now and then go wrong . . . but overwhelmingly the chances are they won't. Mind you, having said that, I reckon the cheapest ones are getting better and better and you can even get very long guarantees with some of them. Good news, isn't it?

So, let's assume you've gone along to the showroom and are gazing, slightly bemused, at a sea of binoculars. Take your time and test whatever takes your fancy. First, make sure you adjust them for your particular eyes. There will be two focusing wheels on the binoculars. One is conveniently placed to be used all the time to focus the binoculars in normal use. It has no numbers on it. The other is the individual eye focus and that will have numbers on it. First, find a distant object and focus on it with both eyes. Then, using the normal focus wheel, close your left eye and looking through the right eyepiece only, focus with the individual focusing wheel. Then look again with both and refocus with the normal wheel if necessary. Make a note of the number you've set on the individual eye focus – this is your personal setting and the binoculars are now adjusted for *your* eyes. If that seems a bit unclear, ask the assistant to help. If he or she can't explain you've gone to the wrong dealer! If ever you try a pair of binoculars that seem not to be focusing properly check this individual setting. It really does vary quite a bit from person to person.

You should then carry out a few specific tests as you look through the binoculars. Basically what it comes down to is: Is the picture natural? It should be what you see with your naked eye, only closer. Several things can be wrong: there may be a slight 'double image' effect; or objects may have blue or yellow edges; the image may not be formed evenly all the way across; or the overall tone may look rather orangey or bluish. Try looking at a dull area as well as in sunlight – is the picture nice and bright? Make sure there's a good wide 'field of view'. If you're happy with all that, check how close the binoculars will focus. It's only in recent years that the manufacturers seem to have accepted the fact that birds sometimes hop closer and closer and you don't want to have to keep backing away to keep them in focus. I once did that and backed over a small cliff! Also you may want to study minute feather detail, or butterflies and insects. So close focusing can be pretty essential. Ideally they should be able to focus down to about 4 or 5 metres, but by no means all of them do.

You may well find that several pairs do pass all the optical tests, and yet some will 'feel' better than others. It's a matter of personal taste; some people like them big and chunky, others slim and dainty. Or you may prefer particular focusing wheels or eye cups (soft rubber ones that fold back for spectacle wearers, for example).

If you do find yourself irresistibly attracted to a £500 pair but your pocket is less enthusiastic, why not consider secondhand, especially if they carry a guarantee? It's perhaps the most important decision a birdwatcher makes so take your time, ask questions, make lots of comparisons and eventually buy wisely. One thing you can be sure of: a good pair of binoculars is terrific value for money, if only for the pleasure they bring you.

OK. So now you've bought your binoculars. Before you leave the show-room, buy something else: quite cheap, but invaluable. A rainshield. It's a little leather cap that slips over the straps and covers the eye-pieces when it's raining, but it is easily flipped up when it isn't or when you're using the binoculars. All binoculars *should* be sold with them – but very very few are.

Your brand new binoculars will probably come in a case and have little plastic covers over all the lenses. You may well be tempted to carry them out into the field like this, safely slung over your shoulder, and only get them out when you need them. Well, you'll miss an awful lot of birds if you do.

When you're birdwatching keep your binoculars round your neck at all times – ready for action. No case, no lens covers (except the rainshield of course). Also adjust the strap so that your 'bins' hang comfortably on your chest. If you have them dangling round down your waist it'll not only take longer to lift them up to your eyes but also they may swing about and give you a nasty whack in a sensitive area. I know this may all seem very obvious, but every time I go out birdwatching I see people fumbling around with cases and lens caps or suffering from low slung binocular bruises.

Even the best and most carefully chosen binoculars may take a bit of getting used to, so do practice as it were and use them under all sorts of conditions, especially during that two weeks approval period – and if you really aren't happy, even if you can't exactly say why, do take them back and try something else.

A final word on the use of binoculars – don't just use them for looking at birds you've already spotted with your naked eye. Use them to *find* birds too – scan around over the mudflats, or the fields, along hedgerows and fences, even through the branches of a tree. It's amazing how what seemed like an empty bush will sometimes turn out to be full of birds when you look at it through binoculars! More of that later (see Appendix, page 192, Top 18 Binoculars) . . . meanwhile, onto the next piece of equipment.

An empty bush? . . . not at ×10!

Telescopes

Not *quite* as vital as binoculars and if you can't afford one right now don't panic. There are many excellent birders who rarely use a telescope. On the other hand, they are super things and open up a whole new world of close-up views and different birdwatching techniques.

First the don't. Again *don't* go to a local chemist or camera shop: they'll have even fewer telescopes than binoculars, or worse still they may try to sell you something designed for stargazing, not birdwatching. Even if they *have* got one or two of the real thing they definitely won't have anything like the range of a specialist showroom.

So *that*'s where to buy from.

The wide use of telescopes is a relatively recent phenomenon. When I was a youngster only the dedicated birdwatchers had one – including me of course! – and we had no choice but to buy a long brass monster with draw tubes that essentially didn't look much different from what Lord Nelson used when he went birdwatching. Nowadays things are *very* different. You won't find the brass 'scopes' anywhere but in an antique

shop but you *will* find a bewildering choice, many of which don't even look like telescopes! Some still have draw tubes (though they are rarely as long as Nelson's!), whilst others don't. Some look more like telephoto lenses. Some you look straight through and some you look down into. Some have a fixed magnification, some have variable zooms.

The one thing they have in common is that they will bring birds considerably closer than binoculars. Unavoidably though the field of view is narrower and they are not so convenient to use. So . . . a telescope is *never* a substitute for binoculars. Which type of telescope you prefer is very much a matter of taste.

It may also depend on how you want to carry and set up your 'scope. It is virtually impossible to hand-hold a telescope steadily enough to observe birds for any length of time. So you'll need to use some kind of extra support. In the old days we used to lie down and prop up the end of our long brass telescopes on our knees. If you could find a nice tussock to rest your head on it was quite a comfortable posture – if you couldn't, it was instant neck-ache.

Some modern 'scopes are long enough to use this method and some birdwatchers still do, carrying the collapsed 'scope in a big pocket or in its case slung over one shoulder. You may choose to do this but remember you won't see a lot if you lie down when the bird is over the other side of a wall. In those circumstances you rely on finding convenient fences, trees or rocks to lean your 'scope on. It's certainly often possible.

Most people, however, keep their telescopes on a tripod. It's more to carry but it's not as inconvenient as it at first seems. You can buy a tripod sling so the whole thing folded up can be slung over one shoulder. This seems to work well for a lot of people although tripod manufacturers don't seem to have caught up yet and most birdwatchers I've seen using slings have had to drill a hole somewhere in the tripod's centre rod to clip the sling on to.

Personally, I find that the adjustment handle of the tripod will hook over my shoulder and stay there – maybe I've just developed a telescope-groove over the years, but it works for me.

There are almost as many tripods on the market as there are telescopes. Two things to bear in mind when you buy one. You don't need as many adjustment possibilities as for a camera. Some tripod-heads are controlled entirely by one lever and this definitely makes telescope handling easier.

Secondly, do make sure your tripod isn't *too* lightweight – otherwise the merest breeze will give you a terrible picture-shake and the whole thing may even keel over. Funnily enough a reasonably heavy tripod with a telescope attached is better balanced and *easier* to carry.

Nothing will be as steady as a good tripod but, if you really can't face carrying one, how about a monopod? You've probably seen sports photographers using them with big camera lenses. They're not bad but not great, and in fact are awkward to carry – definitely nowhere to attach the sling!

Or, again borrowing an idea from photographers, you could try a shoulder pod. There are some that look rather like machine-gun handles which I find work rather well with the small compact telescopes. Again not as steady as a tripod but it can be conveniently slung over one shoulder and you can be very 'quick on the draw' if you want to switch from binoculars to 'scope for an instant close-up.

To be honest I think it depends quite a bit on the conditions under which you are birdwatching as to which is the most appropriate way of carrying and supporting your telescope. For example, if you are watching most of the time from a permanent hide at, say, an RSPB reserve, there's quite an argument for not carrying *any* kind of extra support. The relative heights of benches and viewing slots in these hides make tripods very difficult to manoeuvre. You can buy a contraption called a 'hide clamp' which screws onto whatever wooden ledge is available. It works perfectly well, but it's pretty expensive considering it's basically only a metal rod and a ratchet. You may well find that leaning the telescope on the window ledge is almost as efficient.

In other circumstances I think you'll find a tripod is almost essential – scanning across an estuary or a big reservoir, or sea-watching, for example. (See Sea-watching, page 82.)

On the other hand, I've been on bird-trips where I've wandered around for days without ever using my telescope once. There were evenings I had to have my tripod surgically removed from my shoulder! Under such circumstances, I now use the shoulder-pod set up. What I would *never* do is leave my telescope behind altogether. If you do you'll regret it. I'll give you an example. A few years ago I was filming a TV series down on Portland Bill in Dorset in mid-September. The time and the place were no coincidence. The BBC were forever fixing filming schedules bang slap in the middle of the migration season, so the only way I had of making sure I didn't miss out altogether was to persuade them to film in good birdwatching areas. Hence we shot various sequences in Devon, Cornwall, East Kent – just near Dungeness in fact – and at Portland, which as it happens does have an excellent variety of locations that in their time have passed for anything from the Galapagos Islands to the Himalayas!

Any time I wasn't actually needed in front of camera, I slipped away with binoculars and telescope to see what I could find. This particular afternoon I hit the jackpot.

I was tramping alongside a ploughed field some way away from the Bird Observatory. I decided to scan across it to see if there were any larks, pipits or buntings crawling in and out of the furrows. There weren't. But there was one bird – at least I *thought* it was a bird. Way at the far end, and through a heat haze, I could see what looked like a grey head peeking out from behind a clump of thistles. Through binoculars, I couldn't even be sure if it *was* a bird. Maybe it was a stone or a lump of mud? I switched to my telescope. I had trouble keeping it from wobbling – I told you shoulder-pods weren't as steady as tripods. But it was what I saw that made me tremble with excitement. It *was* a bird's head: greyish on top, white chin, dark through the eye – it looked a bit like a Lesser Whitethroat, only bigger. But most thrilling of all . . . its beak was largely bright yellow. Through binoculars I couldn't even see it had a beak! Even as I lowered my 'scope and began to creep forward for a better view, the bird took off, skimmed over the road, over the hedge, over the hillside, and disappeared. For half an hour I searched and didn't find it. I raced back to the observatory and gathered a posse. For three hours *they* searched. At last they refound the bird that I'd been able to confidently identify as . . . an American Yellow-billed Cuckoo (a great rarity and one that rarely survives the Atlantic crossing). If I hadn't had my telescope with me it might still have been a lump of mud!

Is it . . . or isn't it? . . .

So, yes I really do recommend getting a telescope. Since their wide-spread use *is* relatively recent the state of the art is excellent as more and more instruments are being designed specifically for birdwatchers' needs. Mind you, barely a week goes by without a new improved version coming out and there's a terrible temptation to trade in whatever you've got for the latest model. The consolation is I honestly think I can say that there are very very few poor telescopes on the market, so whatever you end up with it's likely to be pretty good. Also, whatever the claims, I don't think that there is or maybe can ever be a single telescope set-up that is perfect for all conditions.

I'll admit I have two! I use a small compact 'scope on a shoulder-pod when I'm pottering about in fields and woodlands. It has interchangeable lenses but I keep it on a wide angle × 22 which more than doubles my binocular magnification but gives me almost as wide field of view. For sea-watching or estuaries and mudflats I have a bigger telescope with excellent light gathering power and this one I use at × 30 (but I keep a × 40 in my pocket). This can really only be used on a tripod.

So, again, go to that showroom and try them out carefully and slowly. And think about what kind of eye-pieces you prefer, fixed or zoom, straight or angled and so on.

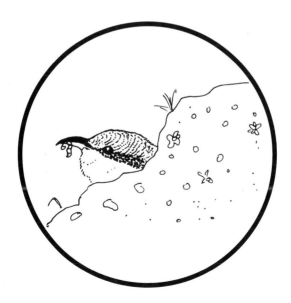

Yes it is!

Even more than binoculars, telescopes may take a bit of getting used to. I have known birdwatchers who just can't be doing with them. They are missing a lot! But it's an awful lot of money to waste, so please do make absolutely sure you're comfortable before you buy. Unlike one bloke I knew. He was an elderly birdwatcher who bought himself a Questar.

Now, a Questar is a very remarkable and extremely expensive telescope. It is constructed on the same principle as a telephoto mirror-lens, and costs well over a thousand pounds. However, they are not quite so straightforward to use as a conventional telescope. First you have to find the bird in the viewfinder at a very low magnification – only about × 6. If you need to scan around, what you see is the reverse of the way you actually pan – a mirror image in effect. It's not easy to describe, and at first it's not very easy to do either! Anyway, then you flip a little lever and this switches to a very high magnification (× 50 or more) and you fine-focus with a little gnarled wheel. The effect is stunning and the picture brilliant. However, it is a procedure that certainly takes practice, though expert Questar users can do it in seconds. It also requires a good sharp eye for finding the bird at low magnification in the first place. Alas, that sharp eye was exactly what this fellow lacked. He was a member of a birdwatching group I co-led abroad. For days I watched him wrestle with his Questar, and for hours my co-leader instructed him how to use it. I don't think he ever found a bird in the first place let alone got it into close-up. Sadly, I fear he'll *never* get the hang of it. Still, I suppose I needn't feel too sorry for him if he can afford to blow a thousand pounds as easily as that!

Actually, come to think of it, something else I observed on that trip abroad. It's true telescopes are wonderful, and it's equally true that these days nearly all birdwatchers carry and use them. Everyone in our group did. In fact, I began to feel they used them too much. If ever someone spotted a good bird, even if it was an elusive warbler flitting in the tree-tops, many people would attempt to put their telescopes straight on it, and often they failed. The bird would disappear and they'd have missed it. The rule has to be *always* find a bird in your binoculars first, and make sure you've got a decent view of it too. *Then* go in for the super close-up. Common birds will look rare, rare ones will look magical, and every now and then lumps of mud will turn into Yellow-billed Cuckoos – oh, and vice versa! (See Telescopes, page 193.)

OK now back to my checklist . . . Binoculars . . . telescope . . . what else?

Notebook and Pencil

Not quite such a bewildering choice here! Funnily enough though, I don't think the ideal notebook is widely available (so here's a chance for some manufacturer to fill a gap). To my mind it should be small enough to fit into the average pocket. Have solid waterproof covers. Flip open vertically as it were. Have an elastic to retain pages and keep your place, and a pencil firmly attached. In my experience the only one that really fits the bill is a policeman's notebook! Many years ago I was fortunate enough to have to play a policeman on a TV show (pretty unlikely casting I admit). At that time the props department acquired a whole boxful of notebooks for me, only one of which I needed on the telly. The rest have kept me going as field notebooks ever since. Until now – I've just run out. So if there's any sympathetic policeman reading this . . .

I dare say there must be some shops somewhere in the world who sell similar notebooks but you just try finding them! Fortunately, any small notebook and a sharpened pencil, or even a pen will basically do the job. Plus, there is now an alternative – the tiny micro-cassette tape recorder. I am, in my old (or is it just middle?) age becoming increasingly long-sighted. Luckily this doesn't affect my birdwatching as I only need to use glasses for reading and writing. But it does affect my ability to take field notes. So I must admit I find myself using a little tape machine more and more. The only disadvantage is that you can't do field sketches on a tape recorder. The advantage is, you can hold your binoculars in one hand and your mini-recorder in the other and dictate a description whilst still looking at the bird. Anyway, if your carefully chosen weatherproof jacket has lots of pockets it's no big deal to carry a notebook *and* a tape recorder. What exactly goes into either one of them we shall come to later!

Whatever it is, it should eventually be written up into a big notebook. I've been keeping these bird-diaries for over thirty years now. The earliest of them are in floppy school exercise books, then for years I used hardback exercise books and it's only comparatively recently that it dawned on me that by far the best system is to use hardbacked ring binders. This means you can add to your own notes by inserting pages of relevant articles from magazines, or extra photos and drawings that can be slipped into plastic covers and so on.

One stylistic note I'd recommend. Many of my big notebook entries are a bit stark. They are little more than dates, places and lists of birds and they do look as though they were done by a birdwatching computer. Maybe I've just slowed down in recent years, but lately I've taken to writing in a much more narrative style, much as if I were writing a journal or an account of the day for a magazine article. I've found it more fun to write but, more to the point, it's also more fun to read back to yourself in the future when you fancy a bit of ornithological nostalgia. Quite simply, it brings back more vivid memories of places, people and birds. In fact if you go off on a bird-holiday, why not write up this kind of diary each evening, on a pad with pre-punched holes, and then it can be slipped into the ring binder when you get home?

Keeping detailed accounts over the years can be very rewarding. Not only is it fun to remember, but the information may be valuable if you can compare past and present records from the same place. Who knows, you might even publish them some day! Mm . . . now there's an idea . . .

But in a sense I'm racing ahead too fast. You've just bought your new binoculars and telescope, and with notebook and pencil poised you're off to see some birds . . . But how are you going to recognize them? Aha yes, we now come to the one other absolutely essential birdwatching item.

On to the next chapter please . . .

Field Guides

I said earlier that there's good stuff available . . . and there's not so good stuff. Nowhere is this more true than in bird books. I'll go further, some of the not so good ones really are pretty bad. Not only are they a waste of money, they are actually very confusing or even misleading. A new birdwatcher can be set off on completely the wrong foot by buying the wrong book. There are just as many good books and some really excellent ones – so let's make sure that's what we get.

First of all, what exactly is a field guide?

Put simply, it's a book that should enable you to identify more or less any bird you might see in Britain, and certainly all the commoner ones. The formats are likely to be similar in all field guides. Pictures of birds with descriptions and notes on how to identify them. So the first step to choosing the right book is to make absolutely sure it *is* a field guide. Some bird books obviously aren't. *This* one isn't! However, there are an awful lot of books in the shops that on the face of it might *look* like field guides, but they're not either. Some of them are big glossy books with lots of pretty paintings and great photos that are usually called something like *A Book of Birds* or *Birds of the World* or *The World of Birds*. They are often referred to as 'coffee-table books' and that in my opinion would often be their best use – fix four little legs on the corners and they'd make nice little coffee-tables with more-ornate-than-usual tops. Or you could cut out the pictures and make a super collage; but wait till they appear at a much reduced price in next year's sale, which they surely will. These books are definitely *not* field guides and would be more honestly titled *Some Birds* or even *Some Nice-Looking Birds*. I wouldn't feel so hostile about them if they weren't often about the only bird books stocked by some shops and if, therefore, well-meaning parents didn't get conned into buying them for their kids who are just getting into birdwatching. The same goes for a number of books, usually illustrated with photos, that, when you look into them, only have a small random selection of species with a text that looks as if it's been pinched from a children's encyclopedia. Some of these look even more like field guides but they're still recognisable as inadequate. More insidious: there is at least one book available, and widely distributed, that does a very good impression of a British field guide and yet is in fact a translation of a Czechoslovakian publication and therefore not only excludes many birds seen regularly in Britain but, worse still, includes some that have never been recorded here at all. For example, there's a picture of a Black Woodpecker with the comment 'Common in gardens and woods.' In Czechoslovakia maybe, but if one occurred here it'd cause the biggest twitch of all time! As it happens it's a pretty lousy drawing of a Black Woodpecker too!

The problem is there are various business deals between stockists and distributors, and so on. I won't go into the economics of why it happens, but the result is that there are very few bookshops that offer a really good selection of natural history books and the ones they do have are very often the bad ones, or at least the good ones are in a minority. This is even more true of the kind of glorified newspaper and magazine shops that also have a small book department. I'm not entirely blaming the shops. I'm sure they feel it's better business to stock cheap foreign translations or whatever, but my task here is to help the birdwatcher, not the bookseller.

So, where should you buy your field guides? Surprise, surprise – back to the specialists! In fact, there aren't many shops that only sell natural history books – that *would* be uneconomical – but at least try and seek out those few bookshops that really do have a wide selection. Or, perhaps more conveniently, do your research first and then mail order. There really *are* specialist mail order firms (see Appendix, page 188). Orders are taken over the phone, you can use a credit card, and the service is very quick. All in all, a very convenient way to shop.

There are several excellent field guides (see book list, page 189) though I doubt if even the writers or publishers would claim that any are absolutely perfect. They do all have the following things in common so these are also the features to make sure of when you're deciding which to get . . .

- They should be small enough to take out with you into the field.
- They should have a full selection of all the birds that occur at all regularly in Britain.
- Each species should be portrayed, in all its different possible plumages – male, female, juvenile, and winter and summer, where it applies (some species have fewer variations).
- The text should have notes on how to identify the bird, its calls, its preferred habitat and so on.
- There should be distribution maps to tell you in what parts of the country the species is recorded and at what times of the year.

There are several books that fulfil the criteria and all of them have some fine qualities. They vary only in the excellence of the artwork, the fullness or clarity of the text, or the number of species covered. It's not necessarily a matter of the more the better. Some guides do not include rarities but restrict themselves to the birds you are more likely to see. As long as this doesn't have any glaring omissions it's not a bad approach. One of the first rules of birdwatching is 'assume it's common until proved otherwise'. The fact is, if you start showing people pictures of rare species they do tend to start seeing them, so to have a restricted selection can help you take a more realistic approach to tracking down that 'funny bird'! Far from being restricted, other guides actually cover not only Britain and all its rarities, but Europe and even the Middle East as well. (Mind you, at least they tell you that on the cover.) But when you see a bird you don't recognize, have a look at the distribution map to make sure it's supposed to occur in Birmingham and not just the Sinai Desert! On the other hand, of course, you'll find these books invaluable if you holiday abroad.

The *Shell Guide to the Birds of Britain and Ireland* has come up with a simple but very effective compromise. You get all the commoner species in the first three quarters of the book if you still can't find your mystery bird, you go on to the last quarter which shows you all the rarities. It's a lovely book – but then so are several others.

There are also, by the way, quite a number of field guides available that have photos instead of paintings. Now, on the face of it this might seem preferable but in practice it really isn't. Strangely perhaps, the camera is capable of lying much more frequently than a good bird artist and there simply are not enough photos available of species in all the different stages of plumage. This is not to say there aren't some very nice photographic guides on the market but I think most birdwatchers would agree that none of them come up to the level or could ever replace the conventional style. By all means buy one to use alongside the paintings but if you only feel you want to shell out for one field guide, I'd recommend you *don't* make it the photographic type.

Anyway, at last I think we can say you are now fully equipped for birdwatching.

Binoculars and telescope to spot them with . . . notebook and pencil to take down descriptions . . . and a field guide to look them up in.

Now comes the difficult bit . . . and the fun!

Good grief – do I really look like THAT!?

Identifying Birds

Let me first of all repeat that there can be a lot more to birdwatching than identification. Nevertheless, it has to be the starting point and I honestly don't believe there's any birdwatcher who's happy if he or she can't put a name to what they see. Certainly it's the question I'm asked time and again by beginners and even non-birdwatchers. 'I've seen this funny bird – can you tell me what it is please?' I'm sent photographs, which are usually pretty easy, drawings which can be more puzzling, and descriptions which can be totally baffling. Some of them fascinatingly so. They may contain lots of detail and yet I still can't work out what on earth the bird is. Why should this be? Well it's not a bad question to start with if we're going to consider the process of bird identification.

You see your bird and you either recognize it immediately or you describe it at first in your head and then down on paper. That's what the little notebook or the micro-cassette recorder is for. Admittedly you could start leafing through the pictures in the field guide immediately but it could be an awkward process, and in any case it's going to be made easier if you know what part of the book to look in, and to do that you still need to take a description, even if only mentally. You need to train your eye and be able to describe and be aware of *exactly* what you've seen. In many cases it may prove easy enough. You'll have a clear picture of the bird in your mind and you'll be able to match it up with a picture in the book.

But that's the easy stuff. The real fun of birdwatching is to be able to put a name to the hard ones as well! Remembering roughly what it looked like won't always be enough. There are too many species that are similar to one another for it to be as simple as that. Added to which, *any* bird you've never seen before is to you a rarity and will be unfamiliar and need identifying – even if it turns out to be something relatively common!

So let's imagine you've seen a bird you don't recognize and you've decided to take a description. What do you put down in your notebook?

First: the date, the place and the weather conditions. Surprisingly perhaps these might provide essential clues. For example, if it's mid winter it's pretty unlikely the bird will be a summer migrant. Similarly, other species *only* visit in winter. The part of the country you're in might also be significant. Some species are restricted to certain areas. And what kind of habitat is the bird in? Certain species prefer trees, or marshland, or meadows or whatever.

What can the weather conditions tell you? Well, they might affect the likelihood of a certain species turning up. For example, many British rarities are blown across from northern Europe. So if you're on the Norfolk coast and an east wind is blowing it may well have brought birds across which you'd be less likely to see if, say, it was a westerly gale.

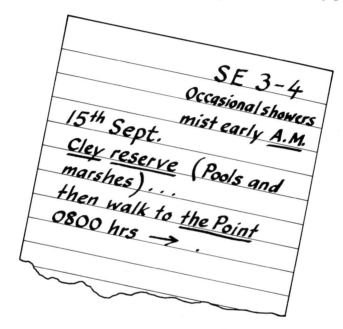

So that's Date, Place, Habitat and Weather. We'll come back to them. Meanwhile: the bird itself.

Bird identification is all, in a sense, a process of elimination. You have to discount all the other species so that you get down to the right one. The first step is to decide what *family* the mystery bird belongs to. Once you've done this you'll already have narrowed down the possibilities enormously. Maybe to one page in the field guide!

Your first glance will give you a general impression, its size, shape, where it's feeding perhaps. Then, home in on its beak. Birds' beaks vary depending on their feeding habits and all the species within a related group are likely to have similar shaped beaks.

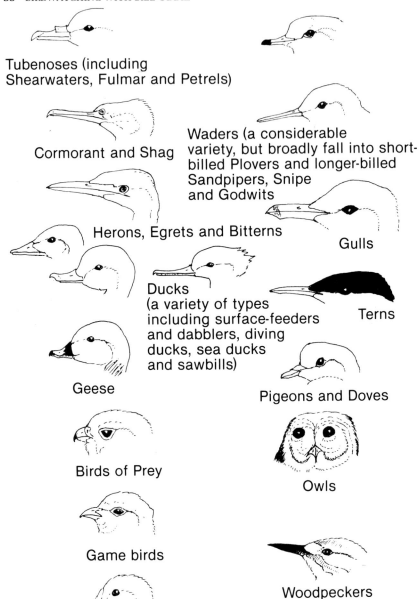

Tubenoses (including
Shearwaters, Fulmar and Petrels)

Cormorant and Shag

Waders (a considerable
variety, but broadly fall into short-
billed Plovers and longer-billed
Sandpipers, Snipe
and Godwits

Gulls

Herons, Egrets and Bitterns

Ducks
(a variety of types
including surface-feeders
and dabblers, diving
ducks, sea ducks
and sawbills)

Terns

Geese

Pigeons and Doves

Birds of Prey

Owls

Game birds

Woodpeckers

Rails (including Coots and Moorhens)

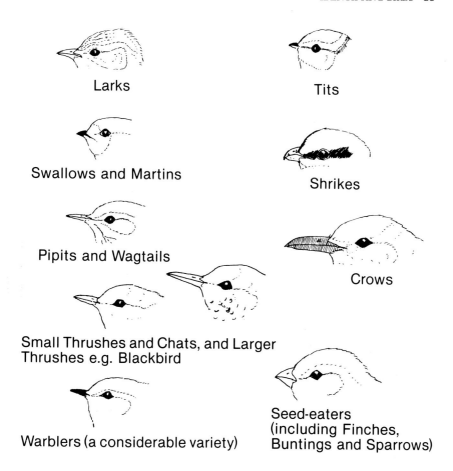

Larks

Tits

Swallows and Martins

Shrikes

Pipits and Wagtails

Crows

Small Thrushes and Chats, and Larger
Thrushes e.g. Blackbird

Warblers (a considerable variety)

Seed-eaters
(including Finches,
Buntings and Sparrows)

NB This by no means covers all the beaks in the bird-world! Even within the same family group there can be quite a range – sometimes subtle, as with the Warblers, and sometimes pretty bizarre, as with the Waders. Beaks vary so that particular species can specialize in certain foods so always try to see what the bird is feeding on when trying to decide its family. If it's not feeding at all it's then that the beak shape should at least give you a basic clue. It's all fairly logical really, for example, with the small perching birds – 'passerines' – it's a fair rule to say that insect-eaters have fine delicate beaks, whilst seed-eaters have wider chunky ones.

Some field guides have a sort of identikit page of basic beak types and if they don't, you should flip through the illustrations and familiarize yourself with the typical shapes.

So . . .

The first step is to try and decide what family our 'mystery bird' belongs to. The beak is 'conical-shaped' – sparrow-like in fact – typical of a seedeater. A finch or a bunting perhaps? OK that's knocked out 90% of the birds in the book already! If you're lucky you'll turn to the finches and buntings and you'll recognize your bird. Not *this* one though – not yet anyway. This is a 'test case'. So let's carry on and take that description.

Size? Compare it with something really familiar – a House Sparrow. Is it bigger? Smaller? This one is about the same size. OK.

'Same size as a House Sparrow.'

Now the plumage. Are there obvious markings or areas of colour? What we need is an accurate description. Where *exactly* are the colours. Phrases like 'above' and 'below' or 'underneath' aren't really specific enough. If the police asked you to describe me in birdwatching gear you wouldn't say 'er – he's sort of brown on top – green in the middle – pinkish face with grey bits on it . . . .' You'd be much more specific: 'Brown hair – pinkish white face with red brown cheeks – brown moustache and beard – bits of grey in it – piggy little eyes – green anorak with RSPB badges' and so on.

Better still, maybe you'd do a drawing. It has been said that the worst drawing is still better than a page full of notes. I think it may well be true. As long as you mark up the bird clearly.

You may care to divide it up rather like one of those charts you see in butchers . . .

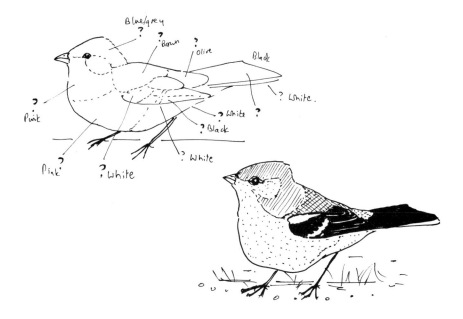

If you fill in the colours and look it up in the book you'll find this one isn't a side of beef – it's a male Chaffinch!

However, some birdwatchers can't draw even as badly as that, and in any case sometimes the plumage and areas of colours aren't quite so neatly and clearly defined as on a male chaffinch.

So how can we put it down in words?

Let's go back to that police description of me. If you wanted to describe my clothes you could do it in minute detail because everything has a familiar name: track shoes, socks, trousers, belt, shirt, sweater and so on. Even if it were a hot day and I'd discarded the top stuff you could still name the visible parts of my body – hands, wrists, elbows, shoulders, neck, chest etc . . . If you wanted to get really technical you could start using the scientific terms: tibia, fibula and so on – as long as you could remember them.

Well, birds don't wear clothes, but they do have feathers and different areas of feathers do have different names – that's the good news. The not so good news is that these names *are* scientific and do take a bit of remembering. It's worth the effort though as it makes a description much easier to take and much easier to understand.

Many of the field guides have a drawing of a sort of identibird with the main feather areas marked on it.

It'll look something like this . . .

The wing as you can see is divided up in all sorts of sections which no doubt seems a bit daunting. But, honestly, it's all rather more logical than it seems at first glance. Just bear in mind first, second, third . . . and biggest, medium and small . . .

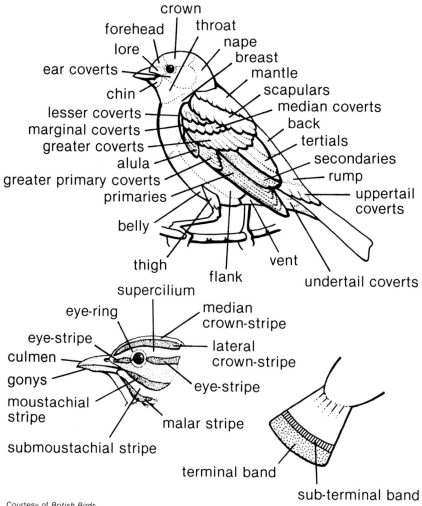

Courtesy of *British Birds*

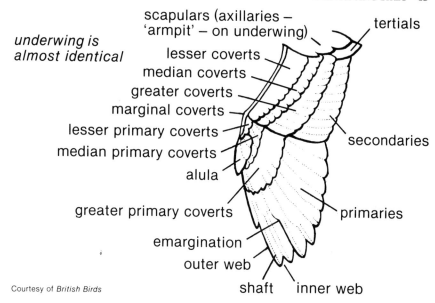

scapulars (axillaries –
'armpit' – on underwing)

tertials

*underwing is
almost identical*

lesser coverts

median coverts

greater coverts

marginal coverts

lesser primary coverts

median primary coverts

secondaries

alula

greater primary coverts

primaries

emargination

outer web

Courtesy of *British Birds*

shaft   inner web

Most of the feathers are really only the more scientific sounding (latinized) versions:

- first feathers on the wing – primaries
- second lot – secondaries
- third lot – tertials
- and *cover*ing them are the *cover*ts:
- the biggest coverts – greater coverts
- the medium coverts – median coverts
- the smallest coverts – lesser coverts.

So just have another look at those identibirds and see how many of those feather markings are pretty logically named. But wait a minute, I hear you protest. It's all very well to recognize bits and pieces on a nice clear drawing in a book. What about on a real bird . . . that may be even moving, or swimming, or flying? You're quite right too. That *is* more difficult, especially since birds come in so many shapes and sizes and not many of them look like the identibird in the book!

The secret is to practise naming feather areas as you are watching the actual birds. To help you here is a guide that I think might be a first for bird books! A selection of photos of real birds with the feather areas marked on them.

In different groups or families of species, certain areas tend to be more significant than others. For example, a bunting's face markings are usually pretty vital, whilst for gulls it's more likely to be the wing patterns. Having said this, when compiling a detailed description it is as well to go down a whole checklist of the following areas:

On a bird at rest
- Head and face patterns, including bill
- Nape and mantle
- Closed wing
- Rump and tail
- Underparts, including throat, breast and belly
- Legs

And – on a flying bird – concentrate on
- Wing pattern, above and below
- Rump and tail, also above and below
- Underparts and face, (which may not be easy to see!)

So . . . now here's a miscellany of birds with feather areas marked. I can't show them all – there'd be no pages left for the rest of the book! – but hopefully this will get you thinking, or rather looking, on the right lines and at the right places.

All the good field guides tell you what the most vital markings are on any particular species. These are called the 'diagnostic features'. So the trick is that when you see what you suspect might be a rarity you can home in on those diagnostic features immediately – which is why you need to know exactly where to look!

However, it's quite a considerable feat of memory to hold all this minute information in your head. So . . . what I've done is add a few notes on the most crucial areas for particular families, rather than for individual species.

It may all seem a bit mind- or eye-boggling, but it's not as hard as it seems, and it really is quite satisfying. Have a look at a few photos, then go out and have a look at a few real birds. It'll take patience, and you'll soon become aware that the condition of the bird can affect the clarity of its feather markings. For example they'll be less clear and neat if the bird is wet, moulting, fluffed up or 'worn' . . . or if you can't get a decent view!

But *do* have a go – it's fascinating and it'll all help pin down that difficult rarity if you're lucky enough to find it.

Pipits and Larks

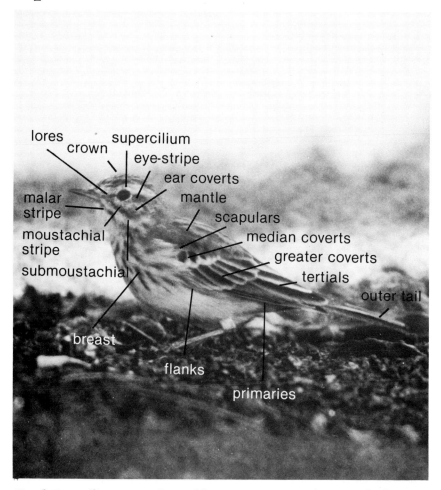

Head *Supercilium, eye-stripe and lores, ear-coverts and moustachial.*
Breast and flanks *extent of streaking and colours, often subtle shadings are significant.*
Mantle *any pale edges, forming 'braces'?*
Rump *streaked or unstreaked?*
Wings *covert edgeings may form wing bars.*
Underwing *(easily seen in flight) may be significant on Larks.*
Tail *outer tail feathers – white or brown?*

Buntings and Finches

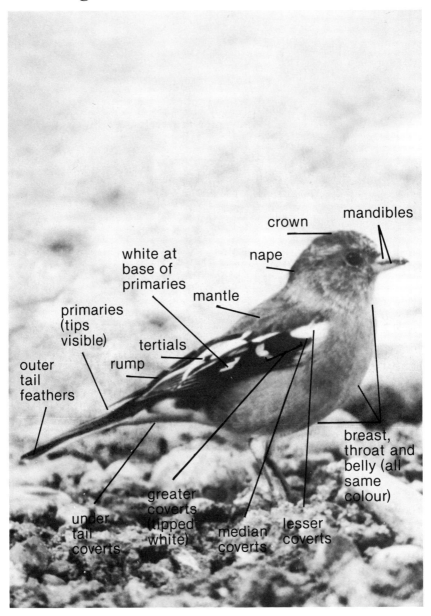

crown

mandibles

nape

white at
base of
primaries

mantle

primaries
(tips
visible)

tertials

outer
tail
feathers

rump

greater
coverts
(tipped
white)

under
tail
coverts

median
coverts

lesser
coverts

breast,
throat and
belly (all
same
colour)

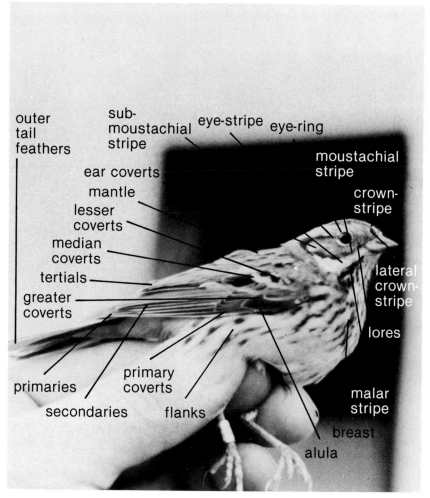

Head *Where exactly are the 'stripes'? – Eye-stripe, Supercilium, crown, moustachials, ear-coverts, eye-rings etc.*
Nape and mantle *striped or plain?*
Wings *tips and edges to lesser, median, and greater coverts often forming wing bars.*
Rump *colour*
Breast and flanks *streaked or unstreaked? How far does the streaking extend?*
Tail *Outer tail feathers – are they white?*

Thrushes and Chats

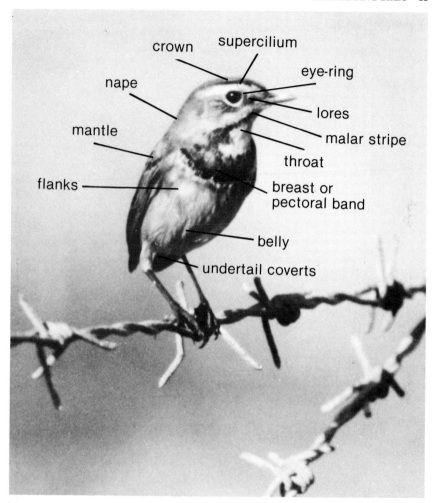

crown
supercilium
nape
eye-ring
lores
mantle
malar stripe
throat
flanks
breast or pectoral band
belly
undertail coverts

Tend to be plain above, and therefore most significant areas are on face or underparts.

Head *Eye-rings, supercilium, moustachial.*
Colour of chin and throat.
Mantle *plain or streaked?*
Wings *Any contrast to mantle?*
Rump *Colour? Any contrast to rest of upper parts?*
Tail *Any pattern on sides of tail?*
Breast *Plain, spotted or streaked?*

Warblers

(remember the points can be very subtle in this group).

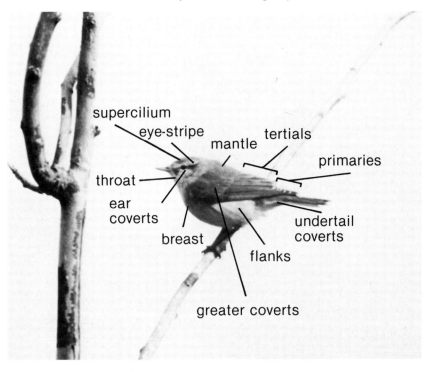

Head Bill – *colour of mandibles.*
Supercilium – length and colour, eye-stripe and lores, eye-ring, crown-stripe, moustachials.
Wings *Any bars formed by pale edges to median and greater coverts?*
Tertials – plain or edged?
Secondaries – do they form a pale patch?
Primaries – length of exposed primaries as compared to the length of tertials.
Spacing of the tips – are they even or are there obvious gaps?
Mantle *Colour and streaking?*
Rump *Colour and streaking?*
Tail *Outer tail feathers and tips – white or plain?*
Underparts – Breast *colour and streaking?*
Undertail coverts *colour, markings and length.*
Legs *colour can be crucial.*

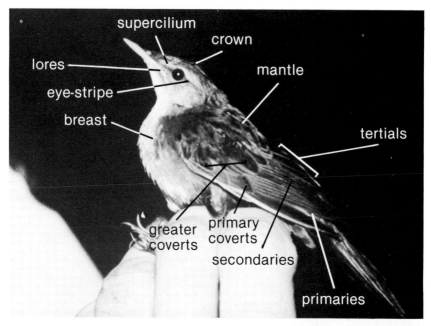

Waders

n.b. the neat feather patterns indicate a juvenile bird

crown

primaries (tips visible) sometimes called 'primary projection'

mantle

eye-ring

tail

breast (pectoral band)

tertials

scapulars (3 rows of smaller upper scapulars and 2 rows of larger lower scapulars)

secondaries

greater coverts (1 row)

median coverts (1 row)

lesser coverts (2 rows visible)

Many waders are fairly 'easy' in breeding plumage but difficult in winter – when they may become very plain and dull – or as juveniles in the autumn. At this time juveniles may lack many of the obvious adult breeding features (e.g. a Dunlin's black belly) but in fact their feathers are very bright and clean. This is particularly noticeable on the closed wing feathers and scapulars which usually have neat solid centres and equally neat pale fringes round them. The photo of the Buff-breasted Sandpiper shows this very well. This is a juvenile in September. It is a vital rule when faced with a 'difficult' small wader . . . first decide its age – is it an adult or juvenile or possibly a juvenile moulting into adult plumage? (See Waders, page 125 and Recommended Books, page 189).

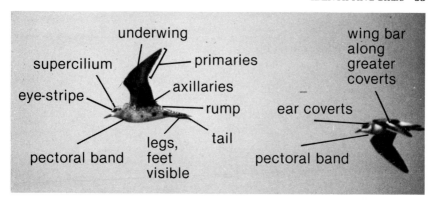

At rest –

Head *Crown, supercilium, ear-coverts.*
Mantle *any obvious stripes or braces?*
Scapulars and coverts – centres and edges.
Tertials *edges, or any patterns – such as pale notches or tips?*
Primaries *Do the tips project beyond the tertials?*
Breast *streaked or unstreaked? Is there a neat pectoral band or is there only slight streaking at the sides?*

In flight or preening –

Wings *Above – Is there a wing-bar (along greater coverts) or a pale trailing edge (along secondaries and primaries).*
Below – Colour of wing coverts and axillaries.
Rump *White or dark?*
Tail *any terminal bar? Extent of white on the sides. Do feet project beyond tail?*

Ducks

*Females, juveniles and eclipse. The breeding plumage males are really pretty
easy!*
At rest –
Head *bill shape, supercilium, base of the bill, ear-coverts*
Wings *scapulars and tertials – shape and edges.*
Flanks *colour and barring.*
Undertail coverts *colour?*
In flight or preening (when the wing is easier to see).
Speculum and speculum edges
Forewing *colour of coverts.*
Wing bar usually along greater coverts.
Underwing and axillaries.
On land –
Belly and leg colour.

crown
supercilium
mantle
eye-stripe
tertials
breast
wing bar
(along edge
of greater
coverts)
speculum
(on secondaries)

wing-lining (coverts)
primaries
secondaries
axillaries ('armpit')

Gulls

Most significant areas . . .

At rest –

Head *extent and colour of the 'hood'; markings on ear coverts and nape. Bill and eye colour.*

Wings *coverts – barred on juveniles.*

Tips of secondaries, tertials and especially primaries . . . are they black or white and do they have 'mirrors' . . .?

Leg colour

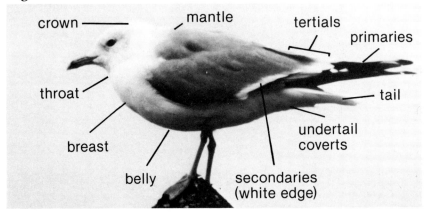

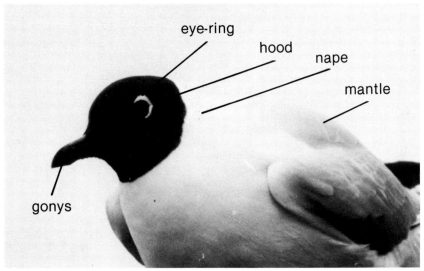

In flight –
Wing patterns *markings on coverts and primaries.*
Secondaries *barred or unbarred? And look for trailing edges to secondaries and primaries.*
Tail *terminal band or unmarked?*

secondaries

primaries

lesser,
median
and
greater
coverts

Raptors

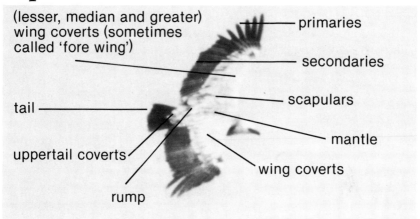

(lesser, median and greater) wing coverts (sometimes called 'fore wing')

primaries

secondaries

scapulars

tail

mantle

uppertail coverts

wing coverts

rump

At rest –
Head *Moustachial, supercilium, crown.*
Breast *streaked vertically or barred horizontally?*
In flight (when usually easier to identify!) –
Underside pattern may be more significant than upper.
Wings *coverts and primaries – any contrasts?*
Tail pattern *plain or barred? Where are the bars – terminal, subterminal, all the way up, etc?*
Colour of undertail coverts . . .
Rump colour *is it white?*

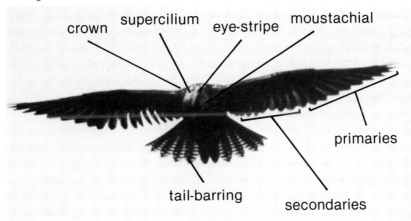

crown   supercilium   eye-stripe   moustachial

primaries

secondaries

tail-barring

By the way, I make no – or little – apology for the quality (or lack of it) of some of the photos. After all, that's the way we often see them! (Not out of focus maybe but moving, which is worse!)

Also some of the birds are indeed rarities . . . but then if they were common you'd recognise them immediately and you wouldn't need to take a description!

For the record, they were . . .

p. 45 Berthelot's Pipit (The Canary Islands; doesn't occur in Britain!).

p. 46 Chaffinch (male).

p. 47 Little Bunting.

p. 48 Song Thrush.

p. 49 Bluethroat.

p. 50 Chiffchaff.

p. 51 Pallas's Grasshopper Warbler (both pics).

p. 52 Buff-breasted Sandpiper (juvenile).

p. 53 (top) Lesser (Pacific) Golden Plover and Greater Sand Plover (below) Baird's Sandpiper (adult).

p. 54 Chiloe Wigeon (An 'exotic or escape', see page 112).

p. 55 (top) Mallard (female) (below) Yellow Billed Duck (Kenya, not Britain).

p.56 (top) Common Gull (adult) (below) Black Headed Gull (adult).

p. 57 (both pics) Black Headed Gulls (1st winter).

p. 58 Sabines Gull (juvenile) with Common or Arctic Tern . . . (I've never really looked at it properly!).

p. 59 (top) Griffon Vulture (*not* seen in Britain!) (below) Gyr Falcon (juvenile).

Now all of that may seem ever so complicated and that's because it is! Well, *fairly* complicated. But don't worry – in 99 cases out of 100 you really won't need to remember or describe any of these minute details because you'll either recognize the bird immediately or be able to identify it from a much simpler description or the field sketch. But on that hundredth occasion you'll be glad you've got to know your feathers . . . (or rather, the bird's feathers).

Imagine for a moment that a Chaffinch is a real rarity. You've seen one. A male. *You*'re sure what it is but you want to convince other people. The bird has flown off so you can't show it to other birdwatchers. You still want to send the record to your local bird club or even the *British Birds* rarities committee. How can you convince them you really *did* see this rarity? You don't have a photograph of this bird and so you will have to submit a full description. On the opposite page is an example of what this description should look like.

Chaffinch (adult male) Observer: W.E. Oddie
15th September 1987
Blakeney Point, Norfolk
The bird was first seen feeding on the ground with a small flock of
House Sparrows. It then flew up into a nearby clump of small fir trees
and eventually away and out of sight. It was watched for about ten
minutes, through 10 × binoculars and 22 × telescope. The fact that the
bird was eating seeds and had much the same bill shape as the
sparrows suggested it was some kind of bunting or finch. The following
description was taken:
Size and shape: About the same size as House Sparrow. Conical bill,
typical of a seed-eater.

General behaviour and movement: Shuffling and hopping gait on the
ground. Flew in undulating style, into fir trees and away with flap and
glide movements
Plumage: Crown and nape blue grey. All underparts pale pink, richest
on the ear-coverts, fading to whitish on undertail-coverts.
Mantle: Warm brown.
Rump: Buff, tinged with olive green.
Tail: Generally blackish, but outer tail feathers conspicuously white.
Closed wing pattern: Tertials black with buff fringes.
Primaries and secondaries: Black with some whitish/yellow edgings.
Lesser coverts: Bluish grey.
Median coverts: White
Greater coverts: Black broadly tipped with white, thus forming a
striking pattern of two white wing bars across the median and greater
coverts. This double bar was also very conspicuous in flight as was the
white outer tail.
Legs: Dull pinkish brown.
Bill: Bluish-grey.
Call: An explosive 'pink' as the bird flew.
Elimination of Confusion Species: Hawfinch would be larger, crown
orangey-buff, only one wing bar etc.

Brambling would not show blue head but *would* show white rump.
Call wrong for either.

Although no other observers were present to confirm the sighting I
was absolutely confident of my identification after checking in field
guide.
W.E. Oddie

Even if you didn't dare submit a drawing (and it *is* always worth it) anyone reading something in such detail could reconstruct an identikit picture of the bird that would be very convincing. You'd also get an extra plus mark for showing that you are aware of other species that could perhaps be mistaken for the one you saw. Confusion Species – we'll be coming back to them later in quite a big way.

Meanwhile let's also have a look at the page from your field notebook for that day . . .

You see you were allowed to write up your Chaffinch more fully later on! Also note that you keep a record of the numbers of other birds you see. That sort of information gets transferred into your big notebook and is fascinating to look back on if you visit the same place again – maybe several times over the year or years.

OK. Let's just recap. How are we getting on with this whole process of identification? Well, what we're saying is: Theoretically, if you get a good view of a bird and take an accurate description (in your head or in your notebook) you should be able to find it in the field guide.

Eventually, you won't even bother to take your field guide with you. Ideally, you'll recognize everything you see. If you *don't* recognize it, then it *must* be really unusual. You'll take a description and look it up when you get back assuming you saw it well, and your notes are full and accurate, you should be able to find it in the books eventually.

So, what's THIS!?

However . . .

The truth of the matter is when you're out birdwatching, and it's windy, or wet, or the sun is in your eyes, or you drop your telescope, or suddenly everything flies away or whatever you're watching leaps into an enormous bramble patch never to be seen again, or disappears over the horizon. . . . Under what are, after all, *normal* birdwatching conditions you *don't* always get a good view. You couldn't possibly take a feather-by-feather description.

You didn't recognize the bird, not because it was unusual, but because you didn't see enough of it. What *then*?

This is the real skill of birdwatching: identifying birds from poor views, brief glimpses, half-heard calls. How do you learn to do it? Well, it's very hard to put it all down in a book. It may be possible to give a few tips and warnings and that's exactly what I'll try to do in Section 3.

What I *can't* give you is *experience*. The truth is, the more you watch birds, the easier it becomes to recognize them. Stands to reason really. You need to see as many as possible – and I hope I may be able to help you do *that*. Of course it will take time – but again maybe I can help there too, making sure you use your time spent birdwatching to the best possible advantage. OK, next Section . . .

Making the Most of Your Time

I have taken part in several 24-hour bird races. The idea is simple. You have exactly 24 hours – usually from midnight to midnight – to record as many species as possible. You can hear them as well as see them. Usually you, me, or the team, are sponsored, so much cash per species. So, the more you see, the more you make. It all goes to wildlife charity. I heartily approve of 24-hour bird races – they raise a lot of money, and they're great fun. I think they also teach you a lot of very valuable lessons about the techniques of birdwatching. You're trying to record as many species as possible in a very short time so it therefore follows that your birdwatching has to be ultra-efficient. The principles that apply to a single day can also be applied to a weekend, a fortnight or a lifetime, but at a much more leisurely pace.

First principle: get up early. The dawn chorus is a wonderful aural treat and as it happens gives you a great start to a day's list as species after species bursts into song.

So, second principle: learn to use your ears to recognize songs and calls. Immediately after the dawn the birds are most visible too, feeding frantically or flying to or from their roosts. Also, there's likely to be less disturbance from people.

For the rest of the day, the third principle: cover as many different habitats as possible.

Fourthly: make sure you see everything there is to be seen in each particular place. This means you are constantly thinking 'What do I expect to see here?' This will help you identify what you do see because your mind is already thinking along the right lines. Also, if you are aware of the common birds, you will more easily spot the odd one out . . . the one that *shouldn't* be there.

Fifthly: plan your day to be at the right place at the right time. In the woods for the dawn chorus, the estuary at high tide, the heath at dusk and so on.

Finally: keep an eye on the weather and be prepared to change your route if it looks particularly good or bad.

All these principles can be constantly applied to your birdwatching whatever the circumstances. So, let's now consider some different habitats and how to make the most of them.

In Town

In your Garden, Backyard, or from your Window

'I never get anything but sparrows in my garden.' It seems like every week someone says that to me. It's *never* true.

Even the humblest back yard, I'm willing to bet, is visited by at least half a dozen species most weeks. And if you keep a list of birds seen *from* your property during a year, I'm equally sure it'll be somewhere nearer 30 different kinds and maybe many many more.

Something . . . over London . . .

Don't believe me? Keep looking up. During the winter you'll almost certainly see flocks of Starlings flying to their roosts in the town centre, and strings of gulls off to spend the night at local reservoirs (and there are four relatively common species of gull for a start). And keep listening – winter skies are often full of the 'chacks' and squeaks of Redwings and Fieldfares (both actually often travel and call at night when the Redwing's high-pitched notes are mistaken for bats!), whilst in summer you'll hear Swifts screaming, House Martins chirruping, Woodpigeons clapping their wings, and pipits, larks and wagtails calling on migration. I once even heard a Sandwich Tern (a sea bird if ever there was one) rasping high in the blue over my house no more than a couple of miles from Central London.

Then how about the birds you can attract by putting out food for them: the various tits, finches, thrushes and so on . . . ? I am often asked for advice on bird-feeders. I always feel like saying 'Don't ask me, ask the birds.' Well, last year I had a chance to do just that! A consumer research magazine asked me to test a selection of feeders. So, for a couple of weeks in February, my garden was transformed into a massive fast-food bird restaurant. Every bush and clothes line had some contraption dangling from it. Some of them loked like space helmets, others would have been hard to distinguish from lumps of wood. The first conclusion I came to was that the birds were perfectly happy nibbling whatever fell on the floor. On the other hand, they were perhaps unaware that their seed might be muddier than was good for them or that the local tom-cat was lurking behind the nearest gnome. Feeders obviously are a good idea but some of them are definitely less efficient than they should be. Several of the ones that were supposed to stick to the windows on little suction pads soon fell off. Some of them had perches or food holes so awkward that Blue Tits were pulling muscles to get at the peanuts. A large number of them were torn to shreds by Grey Squirrels, which I was loathe to chase away because they are rather lovely. If I had to choose a best buy on behalf of *my* garden birds I'd go for the really solid wooden feeders that look like a short chunk of hollow log with a wire grill across it. Even when the squirrels gnawed through the plug they still couldn't get in, but it was great fun watching them try! So yes, feed the birds, but not in summer when the 'unnatural' food can harm youngsters. Also keep a drinking pool open, clean and free of ice; and put up nest boxes.

And why not do a bit of 'bird-gardening'? The tiniest plot can easily be transformed into your personal wildlife sanctuary and not just for birds. The secret is creating a cross-section of mini habitats. Plant a bush or a tree, leave a corner to go to seed, and try to regard weeds as wild flowers, which is after all what they are. It's fascinating to see what plants will arrive of their own accord – seeds borne on the wind or on the plumage of birds. It's also immensely encouraging to plan your gardening to attract wildlife. Certain blossoms entice butterflies and other insects, and a garden pond, no matter how small, will provide a home for all sorts of creatures from dragonflies and water boatmen to newts and frogs, *and* of course the birds then come to drink and bathe in it, no doubt watched greedily by the local cats. I'll *have* to mention them as it's another thing I get asked a lot. 'How can I get rid of cats?' Well, for a start let's rephrase that to . . . 'How can I discourage them?' Now, as it happens, I've had quite a bit of experience at this one. When I moved into my present home about five years ago I found a fairly unkempt garden in which, one morning, I counted no less than ten cats! I set about discouraging them: first by mowing the lawn so that they didn't use it as a communal feline toilet. So that's rule one, keep the grass short. Then whenever I spotted a prowling puss I raced out of the house and shoo'd it away. Actually it wasn't so much a 'shoo' as a 'pisssh' that I suspect may have been a fair impersonation of a large possessive tom-cat. Whatever, they seemed to get the message. I also sprayed the various potential sunbathing spots – especially on the rockery – with one of those sprays that are meant to be

UFOs or a bird restaurant?

unpleasant (though not harmful) to cats. They're usually called something embarrassing like 'Puss-gon': if you can bring yourself to ask for them they do seem to work pretty well. (Ironically perhaps, you buy them at pet shops!) Cats are obviously intelligent creatures and I believe they soon get the message if they are not welcome in a particular garden. Apart from anything else, there are always lots of cat-lovers' gardens available so why bother to put up with the aggro of being sprayed and pissshed at? Anyway, the result of this discouragement is that my garden is now rarely visited by cats, but it is visited by lots of birds.

I've gone on about gardens at some length because it is often there, right on the doorstep as it were, that many new birdwatchers are born. The sheer joy and pleasure garden birds bring to people is immense. Moreover, the kitchen window is a great hide from which to take photographs or study the behaviour of still much neglected common species. What's more, gardens are *important*. Each one is a tiny oasis in the urban sprawl. Put them all together and they add up to one of the richest wildlife habitats we have.

Find a Local Patch

One step beyond the garden – or maybe a short walk, drive or bike-ride away. What *is* a local patch? Simply, it's a spot which a birdwatcher visits regularly over the years. In my opinion, it's the most rewarding kind of birdwatching you can do. You get to know your birds there, you learn how to keep records and statistics, study population fluctuations and observe behaviour, and generally make it your own. Or maybe yours and a couple of friends'. The ideal local patch will have, like the wildlife garden, a variety of mini-habitats within it and if possible it should be somewhere that has not only breeding birds, but also attracts migrants on passage. The key to it, especially in an urban environment, is to find somewhere with a bit of water.

When I was a youngster my local patch was a concrete reservoir within the city limits of Birmingham. It didn't *look* very picturesque but it obsessed me for many years and I saw some excellent birds there. Nearby was a farmyard with a tiny overgrown duckpond, a small reed bed and a clump of willows. That place alone would have made an excellent local patch. If you haven't got a nearby reservoir, how about a park with a lake, no matter how small; or gravel pits, or a sewage farm? An old style sewage farm with open sludge beds may not be the most fragrant of places but they're great for attracting waders and water birds and chances are you won't be much disturbed by people there either! Some of these areas may be owned by the local water board or some such authority, or they may be on private farmland. In those cases do just take the trouble to ask for permission or an access permit. It saves a lot of embarrassment if you're caught trespassing!

The reason the stretch of water is so important is that not only will you find wildfowl on it, but you may get gulls and terns over it and perhaps, most exciting of all, small migrants round it, feeding on the insects in the trees and bushes. Waders, flycatchers, wagtails, Wheatears and so on always seem to congregate near watery areas in spring and autumn before dispersing to or returning from their breeding woods, meadows and moorlands and with them, now and again, might be something unusual. It might be a bird that's quite common in other parts of the country but if you've never seen one on your local patch before then it is in a sense a rarity. I well remember the morning I heard an unfamiliar 'tinkling' over my concrete reservoir and saw a tiny bird drop on to the bank: a Snow Bunting! 'Ten a penny' up in Shetland maybe but not in the middle of Birmingham!

Before leaving 'local patches', a word of praise for allotments. These too can be very attractive to small migrants even if there's no water near them. The habitat within these is often surprisingly varied – there may be brambles and nettle patches round the edges that attract warblers, tall trees for the flycatchers, seed heads for the finches, even mini ploughed fields for the odd lark, or pipit, and those sweetpea and runner bean canes are irresistible perches for any passing Whinchat. In midsummer it may be a bit quiet but in spring and particularly in autumn a patch of allotments is well worth keeping an eye on.

OK, there's the fence post, so where's the Whinchat?

Woodlands

Each different type of habitat has its particular appropriate technique of birdwatching. None more so than woodlands. They say 'you can't see the wood for the trees' and more often than not you can't see the birds either! In spring and early summer at least you can *hear* them, so with patience and a keen eye you should eventually get a glimpse too. The difficulty is that singing birds are usually static, perched somewhere up at the top of the foliage. You might think this would make it easier to spot them but not so, because in fact in woodlands it's usually *movement* that catches your eye. It follows therefore that if it's a windy day small birds are even harder to see amongst quivering leaves and moving branches.

In late summer and autumn it can be really hard because the adult birds are often moulting and are very secretive and, moreover, they've stopped singing. A woodland in July or early August can seem incredibly empty (though it probably isn't). But instead of full song all you'll hear is the odd soft calls and this is probably all you'll get from migrants in autumn too. So how do you spot these elusive birds? Well, as I said, it's movement that will catch the eye – so if it *is* a windy day get over to the lea side of the wood or even of the particular tree you're watching. Find the sheltered spots. Where the leaves are still, the flicking wings of a warbler or the flitting of a flycatcher will be much more conspicuous. Also, remember the birds are feeding, probably on insects. Insects are usually attracted to the sunny areas, so look for the patches of sunlight and the little swarms of insects and, chances are, *that's* where you'll find the birds. You may be given a clue by swallows or martins swooping alongside the trees – look *into* the trees and the other insect eaters may well be lurking there.

You can also try calling *to* the birds. If you hear a call imitate it and sometimes the bird will come closer to investigate. Or you can try 'pishing'. This is a technique used a lot by birders in the USA and it seems to work extremely well on American warblers. It's maybe not quite so effective on British birds but it's definitely worth a try. You make a soft 'pish pish pish' sound – not to be confused with the very loud cat-scaring 'pisssh'! Or you can produce a sort of squeaky noise by kissing or gently sucking the back of your hand. I know this all sounds pretty silly but such noises really do seem to intrigue warblers, flycatchers, tits and so on. Maybe they mistake it for other birds and come to join in, or maybe they think it's some kind of predator (a stoat or weasel perhaps) and come to chase it away; or maybe they just come to have a laugh at the birdwatcher making a fool of himself. It doesn't really matter. 'Pishing' does often work. An extension of this, again pioneered by the inventive Yanks, is to play a tape of owl calls so that small birds come and mob your tape recorder. This can also be used at night to call up real owls who will often answer the recording. Mind you, it's also been known for two birdwatchers to spend hours playing tapes to one another!

All in all, the keyword for woods-watching is 'patience'. As a general rule, it's far more effective to find a likely spot and stay and wait quietly for the birds to come to you, rather than go crashing through trying to dig them out. The reward can be some stunningly intimate views. I recall 'pishing' for half an hour in Dorset and eventually enticing a couple of Firecrests to perch virtually on my binoculars. A magic moment.

Reservoirs

For the less patient birdwatcher reservoir-watching is a pretty good bet! When I was seventeen or eighteen and was occasionally granted the use of my father's car I used to manage a Sunday circuit of the West Midlands that took in nearly a dozen reservoirs in one day. I wouldn't claim that I did them all incredibly thoroughly but the fact is that if you really concentrate, a methodical half hour's scan with a telescope should be able to pick up most of the birds actually on the water of all but the vastest of reservoirs. This technique works pretty well in midwinter, but in spring or autumn and, especially if the water levels are low, you'll probably miss all sorts of inconspicuous waders teetering along the edges, not to mention terns that may only stop off for a few minutes, or small birds in the nearby cover. Certainly if your reservoir is also your local patch you'll want to pay it more than fleeting visits as there's invariably more to it than meets the eye.

Reservoirs come in all types. Some of them look as though they've been specially designed for wildlife: they have gently sloping muddy banks, reed-fringed bays and clumps of willows and alders round the edges. Others look positively discouraging: they have steep concrete banks or seem to be permanently infested with yachts and motorboats. Don't be put off. Remember some of the golden rules of birdwatching: 'Get up early', 'Keep your ears open', and 'Keep looking up'. My teenage local patch, Bartley Reservoir near Birmingham, was entirely concrete and is now even used by a yacht club. Nevertheless, it got good birds in my day and it still does. Many of the best records are of waders which don't even risk bending their beaks trying to feed on the cement shoreline. What they do do is fly across or over the reservoir, usually calling often enough to attract the birdwatcher's attention. You need a keen ear and a sharp eye, but it's very thrilling when you spot such inland rarities as Grey Plover or Oystercatcher circling overhead. If you get there before the yachtsmen you may find some of the waders actually come down for a close inspection of the artificial beach, especially the ones that are rather partial to rocky shores like Common Sandpipers and Turnstones. So do scan along the banks. Even later in the day when the boats are out I've still seen Greenshank dodging past the outboards or terns and Little Gulls threading their way through the sails. A lot of these birds don't stay long.

The quiet corner of Brent Reservoir, almost in the middle of London – Nice isn't it!?

So the motto for watching unpromising reservoirs has to be 'don't give up', and do pop in several times during the day. Also make absolutely sure you've found the best spots. Most reservoirs usually have a shallow end, as it were, where the yachts can't get. It's often near where a stream or small river feeds the main lake, and especially if there's been a long dry spell, it's probably here that a muddy shoreline will become exposed and that's where the waders will be feeding. Also a lot of big reservoirs have a road bridge cutting off a smaller lake or pool. These too tend to be more overgrown with reeds and willows and more attractive to some birds than the rather bleak main water.

It's not only the early morning that can be productive. Many reservoirs attract big flocks of gulls that come in to bathe and roost in the evenings. They often fly out to the fields and rubbish dumps to feed before it's properly light so late afternoon and dusk is the best time to sort through them for rarities (see Gulls, page 130).

The weather can certainly have an influence on what you might see at a reservoir. During a very cold spell smaller waters freeze up and at such times the bigger ones that have ice-free patches may accumulate huge concentrations of wildfowl. Also the east wind, so beloved of birdwatchers, often produces its rewards even way inland. I'm not making any promises but if you do have a period of easterly winds either in spring or autumn get over to your local reservoir and see what it's brought in. Thundery weather especially seems to often bring Black Terns.

Finally, as I said, a long dry period can produce a temporary shoreline, as indeed can the local water authority. I recall a recent autumn when my nearest reservoir in North London was virtually drained for cleaning and for a month it was transformed into an inland estuary with a splendid selection of waders that varied quite a bit from day to day. It made you realize just how many shorebirds do have flight lines that go right across the country.

Oh yes, one last viewing hint on reservoirs. If there's access on all sides it's always worth walking or driving round so that you're not looking into the sun. Suddenly a raft of little black silhouettes out on the water will be revealed in glorious technicolour once you've got the light behind you.

Many of reservoir rules also apply to . . .

Estuaries

Even the most devoted inland reservoir watcher is liable to want to get away to the coast now and then, or you may be lucky enough to live near to an estuary. They are great places for birds *but* they can be an awful

waste of a day if you don't visit them at the right time. I'd admit that the general atmosphere of an estuary at low tide is pretty magical . . . miles and miles of lovely mud, the distant calls of waders and gulls, maybe even wild geese in winter, but just try getting a decent view of anything! On a hot autumn day it's even more frustrating as even at fairly close range everything shimmers in a heat haze that is only exaggerated through a telescope. So, a golden rule for estuary watching: check the tide-tables. (You can phone the local river authority or a local paper will usually have the times of low and high water or consult the *Birdwatchers' Year Book*. See page 189). The best periods to be at an estuary are just before or just after high tide. Actually *at* high tide most waders stop feeding and gather together at a roost where they preen and have a snooze. Often these roosts are pretty inaccessible – out on a shingle bank or a group of rocks. Sometimes, however, you may be able to get fairly close to a roost and find hundreds or even thousands of birds all clustered together. It's a spectacular sight but funnily enough it's not the ideal situation for sorting through the birds and trying to identify what is what. The problem is there are *so* many of them, packed *so* tightly and a large percentage have their heads tucked underneath their wings so that you can't even see their beaks, and with waders, as with most birds, the beaks are pretty vital to sorting out the species.

So the place you want to find is the last stretch of mud that is covered by the rising water, which is also going to be the first area exposed as the tide drops. Obviously if it's a big bay or estuary there may be two or three places like this so you can try one of them before high tide and one afterwards. It's at such spots that you'll see the birds out in the open but gathered together rather than scattered way out across the mud. I particularly like it just *after* high tide as birds come back in small groups and you get a chance to sort through each one before the next lot arrives. Some estuaries may also have fresh or brackish water pools close by them, and often these are excellent places to look at actually during the high tide when birds have been driven off the main river. This is often exactly the set up at many . . .

*Spot the rarity . . .
or maybe there isn't one.*

Bird Reserves

There are of course woodland, moorland and sea bird island reserves but I'm dealing here with what is I think the most numerous kind of bird reserve: set on or near the coast and comprising mainly marshland and shallow pools, possibly with nearby reedbeds and water meadows and also in many cases fairly close to a tidal river. I suppose the best known examples of this kind of reserve would be Minsmere in Suffolk, the various excellent sites in north Norfolk, or Elmley in Kent. Elmley is a particularly good example of the high tide principle where thousands of waders are driven off the muddy shores of the River Medway and take refuge on the specially controlled shallow pools and scrapes of the RSPB Reserve. If you ever go to Elmley make sure you're there around high tide.

There's a lot of advantages in going to these reserves. For a start, everything is laid out so that you see as much as possible and get the best possible views. There's usually an information centre which will tell you what's around that day, and where you can buy everything from a cool drink to field guides, car-stickers, and Christmas cards. There'll also probably be plenty of other birdwatchers around too, so it can be a very pleasant social occasion and even a chance to learn from the experts.

Minsmere.

Mind you, nowadays it's becoming less and less easy to distinguish between experts and beginners as *everyone* seems to be sporting carefully chosen rainproof gear, excellent binoculars and impressive telescopes. Moreover, you can't always tell much from what people are saying as it seems to me everyone gets terribly shy and secretive inside hides! It's not *just* that you are requested to whisper so as not to disturb the birds. I honestly think people get a bit self-conscious and worried they're going to make a fool of themselves by misidentifying a bird that everyone else is also presumably looking at. Well, for a start, don't assume that, just because you're all looking out the same way, everyone's seen whatever you've seen. I have certainly sat with twenty-odd other people and after ten minutes realized that two blokes on the end have been discussing the finer points of identifying an American White-rumped Sandpiper that nobody else had even noticed!

So rule one in hides is 'don't be afraid to speak up!' Well, no, that's not *quite* what I mean. Whisper, but loud enough for everyone to hear if you're trying to tell them you've just spotted a rarity, or indeed if you *think* you've spotted a rarity. Don't be bashful. It's a pretty safe bet in a hide that no matter how inexperienced you think you are there'll be someone who knows even less sitting further along the bench! I'm afraid some heavy birders can be rather gruff and uncommunicative but most

A guarantee of 5-star treatment – for birds and birdwatchers!

Who's watching who?

of them rather like showing off a bit so they'll be only too flattered if you ask for help. There's certainly no shame attached, as nobody would claim that wader identification is easy (see Waders, page 125). Mind you, that's another thing, don't *just* look at the waders. There's usually gulls and terns to sort through, and birds of prey may fly past, and as it happens the most brilliant view of a Swallow I've ever had was of one that had built its nest *inside* the hide! So don't just pop in, have a quick scan and assume you've seen everything. Birds come and go so it's often worth just sitting there for a while; especially if it looks like rain!

Two last hide tips. Again, do get that sun behind you: most of these reserves are literally surrounded by hides so it's usually possible. It's always worth walking round to the other side. And don't forget your telescope, but if you do, or can't afford one, don't be shy to ask if you can have a look through somebody else's. If nothing else, it'll make you determined to save up and buy your own!

Visiting the reserve is one of the pleasantest and easiest ways of watching birds – which is something I couldn't honestly say about . . .

Sea-watching

What exactly *is* sea-watching? Well, it's not just watching the sea, although on a quiet day it may well turn out to be exactly that! Neither is it really watching birds *on* the sea. Sea-watching is watching birds fly past *over* the sea. Why should it be so exciting? Well, under certain conditions hundreds and thousands of birds may be seen passing within fairly close range of our shores. It is a phenomenon of visible migration that can be thrilling both for the number of birds involved and the variety of species. There could be gulls and terns – auks, Guillemots, Razorbills and Puffins – wildfowl and waders, plus the real prizes, shearwaters, petrels and skuas. It *is* exciting. It's also 'difficult' because you have to identify the birds in flight – sometimes at great distances and under awkward conditions – and it's also rather unpredictable – some days the birds come streaming by and other days there's virtually nothing. On the other hand, if you learn to read the weather correctly you can greatly increase your chances of having a good day.

Sea-watching is liable to be best in spring – April, the first half of May – and especially in autumn, any time from late July through to mid-November, with September perhaps winning as the best month.

First though you have to choose your sea watching place. There are some very famous ones. St Ives 'Island' in Cornwall, Portland Bill in Dorset, Flamborough Head in Yorkshire, and virtually any headland in southern and western Ireland. The thing that all these places have in common is that they stick out some way into the sea on a promontory or peninsula. The basic theory is that there are nearly always sea-birds passing some way out offshore but they are usually too far out for us to get a decent look at them or indeed see them at all. Therefore, the further your sea-watching point sticks out the better. There *are* these well-known spots but every year new ones are discovered. Theoretically you should be able to recognize a potentially productive place merely by looking at the map. So if you're on holiday on an under-watched part of the coastline why not try any conspicuous headland or promontory and see whether it's any good? Make sure you give it a fair chance though, by getting there early in the morning, and by keeping your eye on the weather and particularly wind direction. It is almost essential to have an *onshore* wind and a pretty strong one at that. This is logical really. If we imagine those streams of unseen birds out there at sea, they are more likely to become

Mizen head – the very tip of SW Ireland where the land ends and the birds begin!

visible if they are blown closer to the land. It's possible that when the elements are really rough the birds will actually come into sheltered bays to rest and feed. This is certainly what sometimes happens at St Ives when a northwest gale hits the Cornish coast and I've seen the same thing on a strong southerly at Ballycotton in County Cork, where Storm Petrels literally flitted within the harbour walls. Thus the direction of the wind you want will vary depending on what part of the coast you're on – basically westerlies on the west coast, easterlies on the east, northerlies on a north facing bay and so on. It doesn't always work though. I remember sitting sadly on the end of Dungeness Point in Kent one October in a raging southeast gale and seeing absolutely nothing. Even the great seabird experts, who can often predict a spectacular movement, are now and then disappointed and puzzled when nothing happens under what seem like ideal conditions.

What you *can* be pretty sure of is that the wrong conditions will very rarely produce anything. If the wind is offshore and especially if it's a clear sunny day it's unlikely to be worth sea-watching. I've proved this to myself all too often. There is a headland in County Kerry in western Ireland called Brandon Head. I've read many accounts in *Irish Birds* of great sea-watching days there – veritable flypasts of shearwaters and skuas interspersed with rarities such as Little Shearwaters and small flocks of Sabine's Gulls. However, it only *ever* happens on a strong northwesterly. Even a fresh westerly won't do! I know, I've tried it three times and to make matters worse it's been a nice sunny day as well. I've never seen more than a couple of Kittiwakes!

One day though I'm going to be on Brandon when it's all happening. One thing I can be sure of – it'll be a test of my birdwatching skill and patience and probably my waterproofs too. Great sea-watches are rarely comfortable. It's bound to be windy and it's when the visibility is poor that seems to drive birds closer but at the same time, of course, it makes them harder to see clearly, especially if it's drizzling or even belting with rain. So the first thing to do at the start of a sea-watch is make yourself as comfortable as possible with the best possible view. Ideally you don't want to be right down by the water as passing birds easily get lost in the troughs of the waves. Neither do you want to be too high, as you will only get views of the tops of the birds and more to the point you're likely to be blown away in the gale. So, if the cliff will allow it, scramble carefully down some way – and please, I do mean *very* carefully – and find yourself a sheltered niche, behind a little outcrop where the wind isn't quite straight in your face. It may take a bit of finding because remember

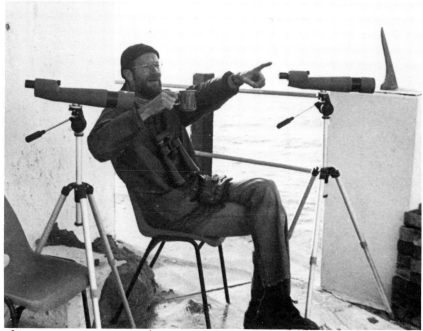

This man is, of course, 'cheating' – staying at a lighthouse, sitting on a chair AND drinking tea!

you *want* an onshore wind, but you can nearly always find somewhere you can sit slightly at an angle. You need waterproofs to wear – including leggings – and waterproofs to sit on, and gloves are usually a good idea. Set up your telescope with the tripod as low as possible so it doesn't shake around in the wind and have your notebook or tape recorder handy; preferably alongside a box of sandwiches and a flask of hot soup! I know it all sounds a bit like an outward bound survival course but believe me it's surprisingly cosy once you're set up. Try to avoid looking into the sun. This is more of a problem on the east coast where the sun rises in front of you over the sea, but you should, again, be able to angle yourself so that you can see birds coming in decent light rather than as silhouettes. You'll soon find that the main stream of birds is travelling from one particular direction – and nearly all heading the same way. So the correct technique is to try to pick them up as they approach and not as they go belting past straight in front of you. This way you'll be able to study them for the longest possible time before they carry on up or down the coast.

If you spot something you're not sure of at first glance *don't* leap straight to the notebook and start taking notes. Birds flying past are in view for a short enough time as it is, so don't waste precious seconds. Watch the bird for as long as possible, *then* take notes. If you're with other birdwatchers try to get everyone onto the same bird. This is never easy but it'll help if you've all agreed certain permanent sea marks as it were – such as buoys, moored fishing vessels, lightships or whatever. Also keep referring to the bird's distance to the horizon. Thus you may start off by giving a clock reference on a passing bird: 'It's three o'clock from the lightship, halfway to the horizon.' Then try and anticipate its line of flight by saying 'Put your binoculars on the red buoy and the bird will be passing it . . . now.' With any luck you'll all be watching the same bird before it disappears for ever! However, the more of you there are in one sea-watching clump the harder it'll be to make sure everyone is watching the same thing and, alas, you'll have to accept that there'll be times when you'll miss something good that the people on the other end saw. Mind you, sometimes *you'll* see it and they won't! Don't expect them to be gracious about it! I've never seen a Little Auk (honestly, never). A couple of years ago I was sea-watching with a friend in southern Ireland. We were both looking in the same direction. He saw a Little Auk belt past about a mile out. I didn't. I still haven't forgiven him and until I see my own Little Auk I probably won't.

And this is what it can be like . . .

I could go on about sea-watching for ages. Some birdwatchers can't be bothered with it at all. I'll admit I love it, especially on my own when I don't have to worry about missing other people's birds! It's so relaxing. You can always keep your interest going for half an hour or so by counting *everything* that flies past, even if it's only Herring Gulls; and even on lousy days it gives you time to think or maybe do a bit of work – I've composed several songs and written great chunks of scripts whilst half nodding off behind my telescope!

On a good day, though, there are few more exciting spectacles nor more exacting tests of a birdwatcher's skill. If you fancy the challenge fortunately there is one peerless book to help you: *Seabirds* by Peter Harrison, a masterpiece on techniques and identification without which no bird library is complete. (See Booklist, page 190.)

Bird Observatories

I don't feel I can discuss making the most of your birdwatching time without recommending bird observatories. Theoretically a bird observatory could be more or less anywhere but as it happens *all* the British 'Obs-es' are on prominent coastal locations or small islands. Thus the range of birding habitat round an 'Obs' usually includes a sea-watching point. In addition, there'll be cover for migrants – often specially planted – and nearby fields, farmland and so on. All of the mainland observatories are within striking distance of major marshland and tidal areas as well. The main point of observatories is to study migration and therefore trapping and ringing usually play a big part in the day-to-day activity. Inevitably in the course of more mundane routines quite a number of rarities are recorded and often caught during a year.

The great thing about an 'Obs' is you can actually stay there. Accommodation ranges from the pretty basic 'bring a sleeping bag and cook for yourself' type – rather like a downmarket youth hostel – up to the superb five star version on Fair Isle, sometimes referred to as The Birdwatcher's Hilton. They're all great value, and I can think of no better way for an inexperienced birder to learn the skills and techniques of birdwatching and, perhaps even more important, to learn to enjoy the company of other people who share the same enthusiasm. Sadly in these days of 'twitchamania' (see page 171) fewer and fewer birdwatchers seem prepared to stay in one place any longer than it takes to tick off the latest rarity, and consequently some observatories remain comparatively unmanned for days on end except for the resident warden. It's a great

Fair Isle – The Birdwatcher's Hilton. Book early to avoid disappointment

pity, and I honestly believe that a birdwatcher who has never spent a week or two as part of an observatory team is depriving him or herself of an experience that is in many ways the very essence of the hobby. Do please try it. And what I mean is, actually *stay* a while – don't just pop in. Funnily enough, several observatory sites can be at a glance relatively unexciting looking, or indeed positively bleak. I'm reminded of Adrian Mole's visit to the nature reserve at Gibraltar Point where he had a lot of trouble spotting any nature at all. Birds come and go, especially migrants, so the chances of hitting a good hour or two, or even a good day on a speculative visit are pretty small. So give yourself *time* to get to the know the area, and the people, and eventually the birds.

Those then are some of the 'richest' habitats. They are by no means the only ones: there's also moorland, heathland, meadows and farmland, sea

Portland. A 'classic' bird observatory. If only the light was still in operation!

cliffs and so on, all with their particular variety of species. I think though that most of the techniques I've outlined so far can, to varying degrees, be applied to all your birdwatching. In the case of the more open habitats – such as moors, heaths and meadows – I would reiterate how productive it can be to keep scanning the landscape with your binoculars rather than merely putting them on to something you've picked up with the naked eye. Mind you, if you're in an area where there are other birdwatchers be prepared for them to come scampering over to find out what you've got if you stare at one place for any length of time.

On Fair Isle they've got rather a good system of driving around in the observatory Land-rover showing a red flag whenever a rarity has been sighted. This prevents wandering birders throwing themselves in front of the vehicle every hundred yards to ask the warden if he's seen anything good that day. If there's no flag it means he hasn't, so please, can he get on with his work? I sometimes think it wouldn't be a bad idea if birdwatchers everywhere could agree on a similar signal – a red feather in the hat perhaps. No feather would mean 'nothing special, I'm only scanning – so don't bother to panic every time I lift my binoculars.' Anyway, the advice remains: keep scanning.

I've already referred several times to the way the weather and especially the wind direction can affect your birdwatching by bringing birds in or indeed driving them away, and it's something that I'll be mentioning again in later pages. The full complexities of how the elements affect bird movements is a major study in itself and rather beyond the scope of this book (though if it intrigues you there *are* excellent books devoted to the subject. For the moment though I'll simply recommend that you do keep an ear on the forecasts and an eye on the charts and there'll probably be times when you'll plan your birding accordingly.

The Birdwatcher's Diary

Similarly, the time of the year may well influence your birding schedules. Fortunately, there are some locations that are well worth visiting whatever the season and in fact it's fascinating to see how the population will change. For example, at a local reservoir (possibly your local patch) in winter there may be large flocks of wildfowl, but in summer a small breeding population of quite different species will be present along with woodland migrants, whilst in both spring and autumn waders and terns may pass through. There are some habitats, though, that are only really at their best at particular times of the year. Perhaps the best example is the sort of wild moorlands that may echo with the cries of Golden Plover or the songs of Ring Ouzels in June but are more or less totally deserted in December. Similarly, coastal farmland may not have much more than a couple of Lapwings on it in summer but during the winter months the same fields are the feeding grounds for thousands of wild geese. I suppose the lesson is don't assume a particular area is no good just because there's nothing there on the day you first visit it – it may be the wrong time of the year. For example, if I were to judge Iceland by my only visit I'd consider it a bird wasteland. Now I *knew* this wasn't the case because I'd heard many a tale of pools of breeding phalaropes and a lake literally blackened by wildfowl. I'd even seen photos. They were taken in June or July. I went in early September.

I was invited by the Icelandic tourist board to join a group of journalists for a quick whisk round Icelandic wildlife. Alas, with all respect to tourist boards the world over, very few of them seem to know much about the wildlife of their particular country. The truth about most of the wonderful breeding specialities of Iceland is that by September 99% of them have gone! Our Icelandic hosts tried amiably to distract us from noticing by throwing up a smokescreen – or rather a steam-screen – of visits to hot geysers and thermal baths, and plying us with some powerful local brew. Apparently this sort of treatment keeps most journalists perfectly happy to the extent that the last thing they want to do is go tramping across lava fields in search of Snow Buntings. Not me though. I defected from the group and set off on a three-day solo expedition during which I found one Wheater, two Golden Plovers, a single Red-necked Phalarope that may well have had an injured wing and couldn't fly off south, plus a small selection of rather dreary looking ducks all in eclipse plumage. I did spot a party of Snow Buntings too, but I skidded into a snowdrift whilst doing so! The country was still beautiful but it wasn't half empty! Some day I'll go back in June.

So that's the message: if you're thinking of going to have a look at a new place – be it abroad or in Britain – do make sure you're giving it a fair chance and seeing it at its best.

Here is a very simple breakdown of the birdwatcher's year. It *is* simple – as the variations could be endless. Anyway, one of the nice things about birdwatching is the unpredictable element, *and* it *can* be interesting to try somewhere out of season when it's underwatched. But . . .

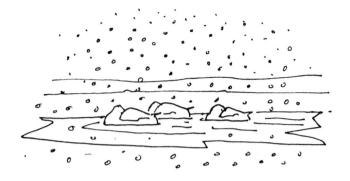

January to March

Peak time for wintering wildfowl on all wetlands. Visit reservoirs and wintering grounds of wild geese and swans. Small birds – buntings, finches, larks etc – often form feeding flocks on farmland or at the coast. Harsh conditions, snow and ice, may provoke visible weather movements – i.e. flocks of birds flying over, usually heading south west to milder wintering grounds.

Regular feeding of garden birds is necessary and rewarding.

April to May

Spring migration. Winter visitors departing but, more excitingly, summer birds arriving. More or less all habitats can be productive at this time but if you intend to travel in search of rare migrants do remember spring is later the further north you are. Thus early April can be excellent on the south coast but it's pretty quiet up in Shetland where the best birds turn up as late as early June some years.

In most of Britain, mid-May is maybe *the* best time and it's no coincidence that most British bird-races are held the nearest weekend to the middle of the month.

June to July

Often regarded as the quiet months when migration has ceased and the birds are busy breeding. This is to a point true and certainly this is the time to visit spectacular sea-bird colonies or go in search of those moorland specialities. However, as I said, early June can still produce rarities and the other end of the period can be equally rewarding as waders begin to return from breeding grounds in the High Arctic. I'd particularly recommend the last couple of weeks of July as a time to check out any muddy reservoir banks, sewage farms or other wader haunts. The birds are invariably in adult plumage and therefore can look pretty colourful (for example Curlews – sandpipers or Knots) or indeed pretty confusing – Little Stints or Sanderlings look very different from the juvenile and winter plumages we may be more used to. Also, quite a number of very rare waders have been recorded in recent summers.

August to September

Autumn migration. Perhaps even more varied than spring, although it does have the problem – or perhaps the challenge? – that many of the birds are in moult or juvenile plumages and may be, consequently, harder to recognize.

All habitats can be rewarding where migrants occur but the breeding areas, especially woods and moorland, begin to quieten down the more autumn sets in.

Sea-watching can be particularly productive.

October

Rarity month! At least it can be if you are at the right coastal location at the right time. For example, a large percentage of British birdwatchers head for the Scilly Isles and are rarely disappointed. Northern areas can be almost as prolific, right up to the end of the month.

Inland though it can go very quiet as the summer birds finally leave and we wait for the big influx of winter visitors. Nevertheless, visible migration does take place overland and I recall at my Birmingham reservoir there was a steady passage of Skylarks and pipits throughout October and I spent many happy hours keeping count of the birds involved and picking up the odd bonus like a Twite or a Short-Eared Owl, both of which looked pretty out of place flying past the block of high-rise flats that loomed over the west bank.

November to December

The winter birds arrive. Sometimes in great invasions, and often at night. I recall November 5th years back when I was a student at Cambridge. As I wandered back into College after a fruitless search for a bonfire, I suddenly realized that the crackle of the last fireworks was being drowned out by bird-calls! For an hour I stood absolutely entranced. The sky above me was obviously chocka-block with migrants flooding in over East Anglia. There were Redwings and Fieldfares, as one might expect, but with them I could pick out Blackbirds and Song Thrushes too; plus masses of Dunlin or Golden Plover and on several occasions the tinkling of Snow Buntings. What I wouldn't have given for infra-red binoculars – there *must* have been something *really* good up there with them. Actually, come to think of it, the sheer spectacle of migration was the biggest thrill of all.

So, as winter sets in, it's off to the reservoirs, down to the coasts and out with the garden bird feeders.

Wherever or whenever you're birdwatching and whatever the habitat, certain golden rules usually apply. Keep the sun behind you; be constantly thinking 'what am I expecting to find here?'; keep listening, and don't forget to look *up* now and again; and don't ever, if possible, let anything go unidentified.

It's all a matter of becoming bird-aware.

OK then, how are you getting on?

Let's assume you're all kitted out with the right gear, and you've been putting yourself around some good bird spots, at the right time of the day and the best time of the year. You've been seeing birds, taking notes and looking things up in your carefully chosen field guide, which as it happens you're beginning to need less and less. Maybe you wouldn't call yourself an expert yet but you are getting to the stage where you recognize quite a lot of what you see without really having to think about it – it's not unlike getting used to driving a car or riding a bike.

It's certainly getting easier and indeed more satisfying *and yet* every now and then there'll be a distant dot disappearing over the horizon, or an elusive flicker in the foliage and, for a moment, you'll feel you haven't learnt anything at all. To make matters worse maybe you have a guess, then the bird reappears in front of your very eyes and turns out to be something completely different. Surely the *real* experts never get mixed up like that? Or do they? Is it really possible to avoid. . . .

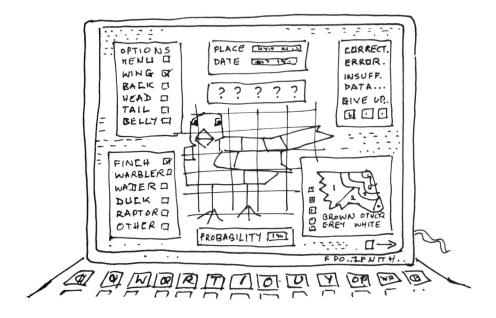

Making Mistakes

Nowadays computers take the hard work out of so many things – so why not birdwatching? How about a pair of 'computer bins' with a built-in magic eye that takes in and processes all the details of any bird they're pointed at and then flashes up the correct name of the species in the corner of the picture, even as you're still watching it?

I bet someone's working on them right now. After all, there are already computer programs on the market that claim to be able to identify what you've seen as long as you feed in enough information, and *that* of course is the moot point. I was once asked to test such a program. It wasn't entirely satisfactory. For a start, I had terrible trouble finding an anorak with a pocket big enough to carry a home computer, disk drive and monitor; and I found having to stay plugged in to the mains restricted my birdwatching range quite a bit too. In fact I could just about peer out of the bedroom window if I risked dislocating my neck.

All I saw was a male House Sparrow and I recognized that immediately. To be fair – so did the computer. I fed in all the details: where I saw it, and what time of the year, the shape of its beak, its size, 'in relation to a House Sparrow' (that was an easy one!), what it was doing and the exact colour of all its bits and pieces. And sure enough the computer agreed with me: 'MALE HOUSE SPARROW, 90% PROBABILITY; 8% POSSIBILITY OF A TREE SPARROW AND 1% EACH FOR SPANISH SPARROW AND WOODCHAT SHRIKE.' These computer programs don't entirely stick their necks out as they do make some allowances for human error, and presumably computer error too. OK though, I thought, so far so good, but anyone can recognize a male House Sparrow – even a Commodore 64 – but how about something a bit trickier? A *female* House Sparrow. I remembered once seeing one sitting on a clump of lupins out on Blakeney Point. I'd hoped it was going to be something rare – but no, it *was* only a female House Sparrow, no doubts at all. But funnily enough, the computer wasn't so convinced: it came up with half a dozen species all equally, or nearly equally, possible including 'GREENFINCH, CORN BUNTING, SCARLET ROSEFINCH, JUVENILE CROSSBILL' and – to give it its due – 'FEMALE HOUSE SPARROW'.

Naturally I mocked the computer for its indecision but then I thought no, be fair, I can learn something from this machine (and maybe it can learn something from me!). Let's have a think about this: why is the computer so unsure? Well . . . *I* know a female House Sparrow when I see one because I've seen thousands of them. But the computer hasn't. Moreover, I've seen lots of Greenfinches and Corn Buntings, quite a few juvenile Crossbills and even a fair number of Scarlet Rosefinches (which are pretty rare). The computer hasn't seen *them* either. All a computer has is *theoretical* information. What it doesn't have is *experience*. So in a sense a computer is like an inexperienced birdwatcher: someone who's maybe got all the identification books and read them carefully – but hasn't yet actually *seen* that many birds.

In the case of the female House Sparrow I'd fed in lots of information but the computer still couldn't decide what the bird was. Why not? Well, because all those species it came up with *share* many similar characteristics: they are *all* sparrow-sized, have stubby beaks, are basically darkish grey/brown on top with no very distinct markings, and generally paler below with some degree of faint streaking. The test bird was also seen in autumn at a famous Norfolk bird spot renowned for rare species – so anything *could* turn up there. So the possibility of a rarity was, as it were, in the computer's mind. From the information I'd given it it wasn't unreasonable that the computer was confused or even a bit overexcited. I could easily imagine a young birdwatcher on Blakeney Point in mid-September hoping to see a rare bird, almost expecting it – east wind, other migrants around . . .

'What on earth's that flitting into the lupins? . . . *must* be something good . . . it *looks* a bit like a House Sparrow . . . a female Rosefinch! . . . I've seen one in the book . . . it *must* be . . . or could it be a juvenile Crossbill? . . . A migrant Crossbill could occur anywhere, doesn't have to be in a pinewood . . . why not on lupins? . . . or I suppose it *could* just have been a Corn Bunting . . . or actually there's a couple of Greenfinches in the next bush . . . maybe that's all it is . . . or . . . hang on it's up again – Oh. It's a flippin female House Sparrow.' Ah yes, I remember it well. You see . . . I *was* that young birdwatcher.

. . . and this is the sparrow.

Nowadays I wouldn't take so long (well, probably not). Why not? Because I am now – if I may be so bold – *experienced*. I recognize a female House Sparrow not really, or merely, by its plumage but by its shape, or even the way it moves as it lollops around the lupins. Birdwatchers call it the 'jizz' of a bird. You can't *really* describe it. It's the essential something that makes a particular species recognizable even when you don't get a good view of it . . . You don't need to see colours really – a silhouette still has that characteristic jizz. If you try to analyse it it's probably a mixture of different characteristics: shape, the way it holds its beak, hunches its back, the speed it moves its feet or wings and so on. But in the long run it's pretty hard to define. Whatever it is computers don't understand it and probably they never will. But people are *much* more intelligent – they learn by experience. Probably the most common reason why beginners make identification mistakes is quite simply because their instinctive appreciation of 'jizz' is still, as it were, inexperienced. I also know it can be really intimidating to stand with an expert who confidently identifies a disappearing dot that to you could easily be a bumble bee or a model aeroplane.

'Linnet,' he mutters.

'How do you know *that?*'

'Oh . . . Jizz,' comes the unhelpful answer.

Please don't be discouraged. The more you watch birds the more you'll learn about jizz. Even I did!

Back to the computer. What else could it teach me? What other mistakes will this inexperienced birdwatcher make? I tried another test case. Again, I fed in the information about the female House Sparrow but this time I left out one detail – I *didn't* put in the shape of the beak. Suddenly the list of possibilities increased hugely: it included everything from a Sedge Warbler to a Rock Pipit to a female Red-backed Shrike! Two points struck me. One was pretty obvious and I covered it earlier in this book: faced with a bird you can't identify, take as many notes as possible – but there are certain points that are absolutely vital and shape of the beak is perhaps the most important. Identification is so often a process of elimination. Once you've noted 'sparrow-like beak' you've cut out so many other species – all those warblers, pipits, flycatchers etc etc. It still leaves quite a few to choose from, but note a few other features and it'll cut it down further, and, before you know it, you'll be down to half a dozen or less. That, by the way, is to my mind what the computerized identification programs can and do do: they'll offer you a short-list to choose from. After that, you're better off looking it up in the book!

But something else I learnt from my second test case. The computer had trouble even deciding whether the bird was a warbler or a pipit or a sparrow. Why? Because I didn't tell it the shape of the beak. But what if I didn't *see* the beak? It almost stands to reason that when you're puzzled by a bird you've seen it's possibly or in fact probably because you didn't get a very good view of it. It was disappearing into a bush or flying over the horizon. All you saw was the general colour, or a distant shape.

It's likely you'll have *some* idea of what kind of bird it was, and first impressions tend to stick. Let's say you saw a little brown bird flitting into the undergrowth and only saw its tail and part of its back. It was streaky.

It looked, at first glance and on that view, some kind of warbler. So you turn to the warbler section in the field guide and find a page full of streaky brown warblers: Grasshopper Warbler, Sedge Warbler or (how about a rarity?) Lanceolated Warbler – 'small and streaky, skulks in undergrowth' – it certainly did that. So . . . what did you see? A 'possible Lanceolated Warbler'? Funnily enough in such cases the computer program might come to a more likely conclusion. Feed the same information in – 'brown, streaky, skulking' – and it's likely to suggest not only Grasshopper, Sedge and Lanceolated Warbler, but also Tree Pipit, Reed Bunting, and . . . Dunnock. Which is much more likely what the bird was. The thing is, by the nature of their layout field guides tend to make visual comparisons only between birds in one family – all warblers together, then all thrushes, all buntings and so on – and often, due no doubt to lack of space, the text stresses the same thing. Thus you'll get Lanceolated Warbler compared with Grasshopper Warbler, and Grasshopper Warbler with Sedge Warbler and so on. They won't mention the fact that a Dunnock disappearing into the undergrowth looks very very like a Grasshopper or Lanceolated Warbler. And it's a perfectly reasonable mistake to make. In fact, it's a mistake even experienced birdwatchers make because, as it happens, not only do Dunnocks and Grasshopper Warblers have similarities in plumage, they even have something of the same 'jizz' about them!

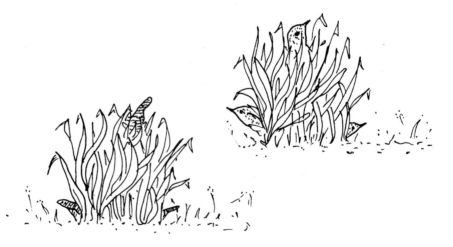

Tails . . . you win . . . Heads . . . you . . . Grasshopper, Lancy or Dunnock?

Is this all sounding a bit difficult? Well it is a *bit* difficult – but that's what makes it fun! Please don't give up. Instead remember this and never ever forget it. *Everyone Makes Mistakes* – even the most expert experts. Moreover, many of the mistakes they make are pretty basic ones – Dunnocks and Lanceolated Warblers again. The reason? Birds in the wild do not pose in full profile like they do in the field guides, showing off their best and most easily identifiable angles. They do leap off into the bushes and disappear over the horizon – and the difficult views confuse *everyone* – experts included. That's what makes it fun too!

So let's repeat it: *Everyone Makes Mistakes.* There is absolutely no shame in it. In fact there *is* considerable shame in *not* admitting it. At the worst, you get found out, and at the least you have to live with your conscience! So, *never* be afraid to ask for help, advice, or a second opinion, and never *never* be afraid to admit you've no idea *what* it was!

So where's all this leading? Well, to the next section . . . I'm going to try to help you make a few less mistakes mainly by admitting the ones *I've* made in the past (and still *do* make!)

But before that: a couple of confessions.

Let's confess – *no-one* likes seeing a bird they can't put any name to at all, and let's confess – *everyone* likes seeing rare birds. Therefore it is perfectly understandable that when you see a bird you don't immediately recognize you start at least *hoping* it's something rare . . . and . . . When you start looking it up in the book, if you don't immediately recognize it as a common species you won't be able to resist taking a sneaky look among the rarities . . . and . . . if you don't find it *there*, you'll be tempted to start believing it must be very rare indeed.

OK. So here comes a statement of the obvious. Rarities *are* rare. Common species are much less rare – in fact, be honest, they are common. You and I – and even the greatest birdwatcher in the world – sees a lot more common birds than rare ones. I'm sorry if this sounds almost insulting but I honestly do think that especially in these days of twitching and 'tick-hunting' there is a tendency for birdwatchers to think rare before totally eliminating the common.

It's surely logical. Even if you can't find your mystery bird in the book at first go, it's *still* more than likely it is a common species. *Then*, you have to consider the reasons why you're not sure what it is: maybe it's a plumage not shown in the book. Remember all those reasons why a bird's appearance can vary: is it a female, a juvenile, in winter plumage, or in moult, half way between plumages, or is it even what's known as an 'aberrant' – an albino (abnormally white) or a melanistic (abnormally dark)?

If *not*, consider what other species it *could* be mistaken for. I said before that identification is a process of elimination. *Whatever* view you have of a bird – no matter how good or how bad – there are only a certain number of species it can be. I know this sounds obvious again but your speed of identification depends on how quickly your very own personal computer (your brain!) can get down to the few possible right answers. It's true, it *is* largely a matter of experience, but you can train yourself to be a more efficient observer by being aware of the possible confusion species, and remember they may not all be from the same family. To give an example: I'd say the confusion species for Grasshopper Warbler should include Lanceolated Warbler and *Dunnock* . . . get the idea? You'll also help this process of elimination by being constantly aware of the *likelihood* of a species being seen in the particular place you saw it and at the particular time of the year. (Remember why we took down such details in Note Taking, Section 2.) Keep thinking: 'What do I expect to see here?'

Thus, if my Grasshopper/Lanceolated/Dunnock was seen in winter – that's sorted that one out: it was a Dunnock (the other two don't occur in winter). If it was in a wood in Worcestershire, in July it's still probably a Dunnock, though if it was on the edge of the wood in a damp reedy meadow it *might* be a Grasshopper Warbler. On the other hand if I were on Fair Isle in late September I'd at least have to consider Lanceolated. Mind you, it's *still* probably a Dunnock!

So time, place – likelihood – will narrow down the number of confusion species. It may seem like a lot to carry in your head or in your notebook but try it on a few birds yourself and I reckon you'll be surprised and encouraged by how soon you begin to cut down the possibilities.

There is, by the way, another reason for being aware of confusion species. It's not just to convince *yourself* your identification is correct – it'll help you convince other people too! Let's say you *have* seen a rare bird and you are sending in your description to the county or even national rarities committee (or indeed, you just want to impress other bird-watchers). Believe me they *will* be impressed if your account of the rarity ends with a paragraph on possible confusion species giving the reasons why you can discount them. (Remember that Chaffinch description on page 61.)

So . . . let's just have a quick recap: here are the basic stages you should go through if you see an unfamiliar bird.

First: Get as good a look as you can.

Then: Take notes, or remember as much as you can. Pay special attention to the shape of the beak, feeding behaviour and general shape and try to decide what *family* it belongs to.

Then: Note the most obvious plumage features, especially areas of colour or conspicuous markings. Pay special attention to head markings, wings, rump and tail.

Listen: for any song or calls.

Also note: Where was it? What part of the country? What kind of habitat? And when? What time of the year?

Then, when you look it up in the book: Turn to the family or families you think the bird belongs to. Look at the *common* birds.

If the shape seems right but you can't recognize the plumage. Consider is it female, juvenile, winter, in moult – or some plumage not illustrated?

If you still can't find it try confusion species in other families. Still stick with the common ones.

But if you *still* can't find it try the rarities!

If you're *still* not sure, try going through the book saying what it definitely *wasn't*! What are you left with? Anything? Well, if you *still* can't find it . . . you've either bought the wrong field guide, or it's an escape from an aviary or a zoo, or it's a first for Britain!

However let's assume you have, at last, found it. Finally ask yourself: '*Should* it be there?' Check the time and the place. Field guides tell you whether it's a summer or winter visitor, and the type of habitat the species favours, and there are distribution maps showing the range of the species at various seasons of the year. Do use them.

One little cautionary thought to keep in the back of your mind though: occasionally birds turn up at odd times and in odd places and that's

exactly what can confuse a birdwatcher. I remember a puzzled group discussing what on earth the strange waterbird could be, wading in the marshy pool in front of a hide at Minsmere. In fact, it was a homing pigeon! No-one recognized it at first because it wasn't on a roof of a loft where it *should* have been!

OK then, here we go – on to the next section . . . at last!

What follows is *not* meant to be any kind of field guide, and in fact I won't even be mentioning *all* the species in the systematic lists. These are bits and pieces that I hope will help, based, as I said, on my own experience of getting it right . . . and getting it wrong. I apologize now for what's missing and quite accept that other birders won't agree with some of the points I make – we do see some things differently (another thing that makes it fun!)

I suggest you use my comments *alongside* whatever field guide you use – they may just help you sort your way through it if you've seen a bird you're not sure of. You may also fancy having a browse through before you go out next time and it may just put a few things in your mind that will help as that possible rarity flits frustratingly away over the tree tops. Oh yes . . . two last general rules that are *nearly* always true:

'Anything *can* turn up anywhere – but it usually doesn't!'
and
'If you're not sure – it probably isn't (a rarity, that is).'
Right then . . . here goes . . .

. . . *but sometimes it does . . . and it is.*

The Birds

The species in these notes are in the same order you'll find in most field guides but, as I said, don't expect *everything* to be listed. After all there are quite a few birds that are totally unmistakable – well, almost. That's a relief isn't it?

DIVERS: Red-throated, Black-throated and Great Northern

Red-throated and Black-throated Divers nest on lonely lochs way up in the north of Scotland. Unless you visit the remote breeding grounds, your best chance of seeing a diver is on the sea, particularly an estuary, or maybe on a reservoir or gravel pit inland. It will almost certainly be in winter and the birds will therefore be in winter plumage which in all cases is basically black above and white below. Divers are not common, especially inland, so the first question to ask yourself is – are you *sure* it's a diver? There are several possible confusion species.

Cormorant: Very easily mistaken for a diver. Much the same size and many of them are whitish below. They tend to swim lower in the water with often only the neck and head visible and have thinner more hooked beaks. They are not uncommon on inland waters as well as on the coast. **The Shag** is similar and therefore also confusable with a diver but Shags are very rare inland. Both Cormorants and Shags can look very diver-like in flight also, though they are less sleek and have heavier wingbeats.

Great Crested Grebes are also black and white in winter and, though they are slimmer and smaller than divers, beware of distant views on misty or foggy days when birds appear bigger than they really are. Female Goosander and mergansers in fact have brown heads but if the light is poor and they are at a distance they too can appear pretty colourless and slightly diver-like. Divers inland are usually solitary so . . . if you think you've seen more than one on a lake – think again!

On the sea in winter, however, you do occasionally get small parties of divers – usually Red-throats – and very ocasionally quite big flocks. So if you hear of a flock of divers on an estuary it doesn't necessarily mean someone's made a mistake – they might *not* be Great Crested Grebes!

Telling winter-plumage divers from one another isn't easy. Study the books and the birds but please don't worry if now and again there's one or two you can't be sure of. Experts have trouble sometimes. One word of warning: the rare White-billed Diver is very rare – don't get overexcited by Great Northern Divers that have almost totally whitish bills! Look closely and you'll see the top ridge, or culmen, is dark and the beak is a different shape from the White-billed.

Summer plumage Divers do occasionally occur away from breeding grounds, and look darker, so beware of the Cormorant/Shag confusion. Even the Red-throat's red throat looks blackish in most lights.

LARGER GREBES: Great Crested and Red-necked

Great Crested is by far the commoner and can be seen on all kinds of water – including the sea – at all times of the year. Even at a distance and resting with their heads tucked away their white breasts stand out a mile. As I've already mentioned you just *could* mistake a winter Great Crested for a diver. A flying Great Crested can also be a bit of a shock the first time you see one – we're so used to seeing them swimming! They are great long stretched out things with whirring wings skimming across the water – a very odd sight.

Red-necked Grebes only occur in winter, usually single birds on inland waters or on the sea. They are pretty uncommon so if you think you've seen one, double check.

SMALLER GREBES: Black-necked, Slavonian and Dabchick

Inland birdwatchers regularly visiting reservoirs are constantly hoping for a stray diver or one of the rarer grebes and I well recall when I was a youngster allowing optimism to cloud my judgement, and my eyesight!

Just as every Cormorant was a possible diver, so every distant Dabchick (the name I prefer for the Little Grebe) was a hopeful Slav or Black-necked! Never forget, Dabchick is the common one and a small grebe is therefore *most likely* to be a Dabchick. The two rare ones are slimmer, longer necked and, in winter plumage, black and white. *But* beware that in winter Dabchicks can also look surprisingly black and white and they don't always have that characteristic puff-ball look. Juvenile Coot also look rather like rare grebes – they're black and white too but not at the

Unlikely, but it could happen.
The one on the left is the Coot.

same time of the year. If it's summer or early autumn it's much more likely to be a young Coot than a winter plumaged Black-necked/Slav Grebe! Female **Ruddy Ducks** (not numerous but seen all the year) and female or young **Smew** (known as 'brownheads', pretty rare and only seen in winter) can also be mistaken for small grebes, especially when seen at a distance.

Slavonian and Black-necked Grebes do occur in breeding plumage now and again but they are not at all common and are luckily pretty distinctive. Moulting birds, though, need to be carefully distinguished from Dabchicks.

GANNET

Gannets breed in big colonies on sea cliffs, in the north of Britain. See them there and you'll have no problem – there are thousands of them all together! However, a single Gannet flying by on a sea-watch is a different matter! An adult is pretty much unmistakable – dazzlingly white with long wings tipped with black – but younger birds go through a confusing range of plumages from black to white and all stages in between. Because they glide on stiffened wings I have known Gannets mistaken for large **shearwaters** and **albatrosses**, and because they sometimes soar up high and flap unevenly dark birds can also look like **skuas**. A young Gannet sitting on the water could even be mistaken for a **diver**, and since one of their local names is 'Solan Goose' one has to accept that a distant string of Gannets flying by also looks a bit like a skein of **geese**! So, all in all it's not a bad rule for sea-watching to say, before you start claiming any large uncommon sea bird – are you absolutely *sure* it wasn't a Gannet?

FULMAR

Another sea bird that can cause problems flying past. It too flies on very stiff wings and is often mistaken for a **shearwater** – especially the rare

Cory's or Great. In good light, a Fulmar is as pale as a Common Gull but whilst sea-watching you often have no choice but to look into the sun and under such conditions Fulmars (and indeed **gulls**) can look worryingly dark. So another good sea-watching rule, if you think you've got a large shearwater – are you sure it's not a Fulmar? Which brings us to

SHEARWATERS

Just as reservoir watchers hope for divers and rare grebes, sea-watchers hope for Shearwaters. Your chances of seeing them are very much affected by the time of the year and even more by what part of Britain's coastline you're on. Only Manx Shearwaters nest in Britain and all the colonies are on islands off our west coast or across in Ireland. In these areas during the breeding season you'll see 'Manxies' skimming over the sea especially early morning and late evenings (they go to their burrows at night and feed well out to sea during the main part of the day).

Otherwise it's a matter of scanning the waves from one of the country's various sea-watching points, usually a headland sticking some way out in the ocean. (See Sea-Watching, page 82.)

Remember the general seasonal rules – shearwaters are pretty uncommon in winter. Spring and especially late summer and autumn are the best times.

Manxies are by far the commonest and easiest to identify since they are starkly black and white. It's possible that a passing **auk** – Razorbill or Guillemot – could be confused momentarily but they flap frantically all the time and never bank and glide like a Manxie. Only the very rare Little Shearwater is said to have a slightly auk-like flight. The other rare shearwaters are all bigger than Manxies. **Sooty Shearwaters**, as the name implies, are more or less dark all over. So beware those dark young **Gannets** and dark **Arctic Skuas**. (Skuas don't glide.) Great and Cory's are not always easy to tell from one another – study the birds and the books – but first, are you sure your Great isn't a Gannet or your Cory's a Fulmar?

PETRELS: Leach's and Storm

Even more than shearwaters, petrels away from breeding grounds are very rarely seen on sea-watches and then usually at a frustrating distance. Beware **House Martins** which sometimes migrate off the coast and skim low over the waves showing a white rump reminiscent of a Storm Petrel.

Leach's Petrel wondering what it's doing at an unsightly Staffordshire reservoir . . . and why hasn't that Black Tern flown south by now!?

Leach's Petrels are rather less black and white and have a more buoyant flight which reminds me of a **Black Tern**. So beware Black Terns out at sea. Moreover, Leach's do sometimes occur inland in late autumn especially after strong winds. So if you hear of what sounds like a winter plumaged Black Tern fluttering round a reservoir in early November – go and check it out! It might well *tern* out to be a Leach's Petrel!

SHAGS AND CORMORANTS

We've already had the warning: both can look like **divers**. Also, a flock of Cormorants in flight often takes up a V formation and can easily be mistaken for **geese**. And they *do* fly over high up in the sky. Telling Shags from Cormorants is not *that* easy . . . but here are a couple of rules to bear in mind.

Inland, it's *much* more likely to be Cormorants, whilst on the coast if there's a really big flock of them, especially near cliffs, they're almost certainly Shags.

THE HERON FAMILY

Common or **Grey Herons** are commoner than a lot of non-birdwatchers think. It seems like every week someone stops me on the streets of London and excitedly tells me 'I saw a heron flying over my house last weekend. Is it unusual?' Well, the truth is there are quite a few herons that live and breed in London and other cities and seeing them flying over is really only a matter of 'keep looking up'! They can be mistaken for large **birds of prey**, and not just by people! Smaller birds, including crows, usually chase or 'mob' herons as they fly across and in fact it may be the attendant screeching and cawing that attracts your attention.

Herons *are* big birds but not as big as **Cranes** which are really huge, fly with their necks outstretched and are *extremely* rare. So if anything really big soars over *your* house – chances are it's a heron!

There are also various rare herons and egrets and the very localized Bittern and Spoonbills. Generally speaking they fall into categories of brownish ones and white ones. The white ones shouldn't cause much problem – especially the Spoonbill (why can't all birds be that easy?). Brown ones need more care and any of them could be mistaken for large **birds of prey** if seen fleetingly. I recall a report of a 'huge brown owl being chased by seagulls' that turned out to be a Purple Heron. Oh and talking of Purple Herons, if you've heard there's one at Minsmere and you go looking for it . . . don't forget Bitterns can fly – so double check!

Heron being mobbed. Easy enough to recognize close up, but way up overhead . . . ?

SWANS: Mute, Whooper and Bewick's

Surely no-one could mistake a swan? Well, it depends how you see it. If you're scanning across heat hazy marshland looking for the Spoonbill you heard was there yesterday, and there's a Mute Swan feeding with its head down hidden behind the reeds. . . . Believe me, it happens. Also there are quite a few big white geese around that have strayed from their farms.

But, yes, swans *are* pretty easy to tell from other birds. To tell from one another though is not so simple. Remember wild swans (Bewick's and Whoopers) only visit us in winter and generally favour regular wintering grounds. Strays do occur though, so if you see a party of swans flying across town or countryside are they Mute or wild? Without a good view it's not that easy as the Mute's bent neck is straightened out in flight. Concentrate on those beaks – can you spot the yellow of the wild species? On the other hand they might be young birds in which case *all* the beaks are pinkish. Don't despair. Keep your ears open. Mute Swans really are mute (well they wheeze a bit sometimes) but their wings whistle. Wild swans' wings are silent but the birds rarely are: both species give beautiful eerie bugling calls and chances are if you see them flying you'll hear them too, even at a distance.

Telling Bewick's from Whoopers? – back to the field guide please.

WILDFOWL IN GENERAL: Escapes, Hybrids and Exotics

As if ducks and particularly geese weren't difficult enough to identify already, the situation is further complicated by the fact that various impostors are flying around apparently wild! They have usually escaped from a farmyard, a zoo or a collection and in some cases have bred and become so successful over the years that they have now been accepted as honorary British citizens! The familiar Canada Goose was brought over from Canada and USA during the last century and kept in parks, some escaped, and now they're everywhere. Back in the late fifties a few American Ruddy Ducks strayed from the Wildfowl Trust, and they're doing pretty well too. The beautiful Chinese Mandarins are also now officially accepted and so is the Egyptian Goose. Such once foreign species can have gone wild, become British, and are now 'tickable' by birdwatchers.

What is more confusing is that there are tame versions of native species swimming around behaving as if they are wild. These include a variety of commoner geese including Greylags, Pinkfeet and Barnacles, and rare birds such as Snow Geese and Lesser Whitefronts, that if they occurred as genuinely wild individuals would draw crowds of admiring twitchers. The same applies to various ducks: who's to know if the Ferruginous Duck or Red-crested Pochard on the local reservoir is wild or an escape?

All one can do is look for tell-tale signs. Most of our genuinely scarce wildfowl would be winter visitors. So if an apparent rarity turns up let's say later than April or before October – it should be viewed with some suspicion.

Genuinely wild geese are devoted to certain areas of coastal Britain. So if, say, a Barnacle or a Pinkfoot appears on an inland reservoir or park lake it's probably an escape. Especially if it stays a long time. Unusual tameness is usually a bit of a give away – wild birds don't normally take bread from your hand! But conversely it's a mistake to assume that because a bird seems nervous and flies off when approached then it must be wild. Look out for signs of wing-clipping. Birds from collections probably had their primary feathers removed or cut back so they couldn't fly away. Eventually though the feathers did grow back and off the bird went, but those primaries may still look rather uneven or shorter than they should be – a pretty sure sign of an escape. Is the bird wearing a ring? Obviously some wild birds *have* been ringed too but *all* captive birds *should* have been, and especially look for coloured rings – another likely sign of captive origin.

With British escapes at least it's not usually difficult to identify what species they are. Unfortunately, it's often much more difficult with exotics and hybrids. Exotics are what the name implies: completely foreign birds, sometimes very colourful and distinctive, that have escaped from a wildfowl collection. They are not species on the British list and probably never will be: Bar-headed Goose, Chiloe Wigeon, Bahama Pintail – I've seen them all flying free and upsetting birdwatchers. Add the common farmyard defectors such as Muscovy Ducks and Khaki Campbells. Then to really confuse us the Khaki Campbells get together with wild Mallards and produce some dreaded hybrids that look like neither or both ... and if *that* isn't confusing enough ... two wild species sometimes hybridize as well, so you get a cross between say a Pochard and a Tufted that the twitchers try hard to turn into a first for Britain.

Fortunately, several modern field guides recognize the problem and include a page or two of these fake wildfowl, but they can't show them

Let's just hope it never happens!

all, especially the hybrids as not even the ducks know how they're going to turn out!

All the birdwatcher can do is remember that such creatures exist and are even now flying amongst us. So . . . here's a good rule, if you think you've seen a rare duck or goose – are you sure it's not an escape, an exotic or a hybrid?

Phew . . . let's get back to real wildfowl . . .

GEESE

Only two species of geese breed in Britain: **Canada Geese** and **Greylag Geese** – so if you see geese in summer they are either of these two species, or escapes. On the ground, Canada Geese are easy enough to recognize. Greylags, however, belong to that confusing group known as 'grey geese' and are not so easy. *All* geese are difficult to identify in flight. Although genuinely wild geese are winter visitors and favour traditional coastal wintering grounds they do sometimes fly across the country and may even be seen over inland towns and cities. Generally, but not always, they will be flying in the typical well known V-formation often assumed to be characteristic only of geese. Beware! Several other species fly in a V and are consequently easily and often mistaken for geese. Most likely are *large gulls* leaving or going to their roosts. Their wing beats are slow and their formation very goose-like and the fact that the light is likely to be dusky won't help! **Cormorants** also fly in a V and are also as big as geese, and **Curlews**, usually near the coast, could also be mistaken at a distance.

On the other hand of course you may well be lucky and see a genuine skein of wild geese flying over town. Which ones? Well first, make sure they're not just Canadas – the *higher* they're flying the less likely they are to be Canadas, which are usually just moving from lake to lake within the city. If they're grey geese they'll probably be **Whitefronts**, **Greylags** or

Pinkfeet, perhaps influenced by what part of the country you live in. Check those maps and keep your ears open for their calls. Though I must admit I don't think any field guide can adequately write down a phonetic rendering of a goose call! But there are tapes and records available.

There are also two species of 'black geese' in Britain. Neither are at all frequent in or over land. **Brents** are now happily very numerous at various sites round the south and east costs. A big flock is unmistakable but a small group or a single bird flying at a distance could be overlooked as a large duck. Brents are small. **Barnacles** are only at all numerous at their traditional Scottish and Irish haunts, and there's a few most years in East Anglia . . . anywhere else, you've either got lucky or an escape!

DUCKS

There are several species of duck that breed in Britain, albeit in relatively small numbers. Much larger numbers spend the winter with us, and they begin arriving in autumn. At this time, most of them are in what's known as an 'eclipse' plumage. Those nice distinctive easily recognized drakes lose their colours and they can look very odd. Add to this the fact that the females, by and large, look pretty drab all the year and you'll appreciate that duck identification during late summer and autumn can be quite a tricky business. On the other hand it's a jolly good time to practise your

Against the sun, no colours, but there are still five identifiable species here and none of them is a Mallard. Look at head and tail shapes, and 'little white bits' when birds are in eclipse. (OK it's Teal, Wigeon, Gadwall, Pintail and Shoveler; but which is which?).

eye for jizz, shapes and silhouettes. Also look out for those few telltale distinctive marks that don't disappear in moult – for example, the white speculum on a **Gadwall** or the pale forewing on a **Garganey**.

Generally the best field guides are extremely well illustrated so I won't go into all the various distinctions between one duck species and another. In fact when the birds are in full plumage – which is most of the winter and throughout spring – it's not a very difficult group to sort out. Moreover, by and large, most ducks are recognizable as ducks. However, there are a few possible confusions and one of them occurs under those ever-difficult circumstances – sea-watching!

During a good sea-watch all sorts of birds fly by – not just Fulmars, and gulls and shearwaters – there may also be flocks of waders and flocks of ducks and individuals too. There could be several different species and certainly not just so-called 'sea-ducks'. Especially in late autumn, parties of Teal dash across the horizon and being small and fast can easily be mistaken for waders. Bulkier species, the **Mallard** or **Eider** and scoters, could pass for distant **Brent Geese**. Overall it's not a *big* problem – but whilst sea-watching it's worth bearing in mind.

Otherwise, here's just a few notes on duck problems that I have encountered and indeed suffered myself over the years!

Shelduck: the big one, which really looks as if it ought to be a goose. In silhouette they can indeed look like **geese**. Once you see their black and white plumage though there's not a lot you could confuse a Shelduck with.

Ruddy Ducks: both male and female have whitish faces, they are small and dive frequently making it sometimes hard to get a decent look at them – at a distance they could be mistaken for **small grebes**.

Tufted/Scaup/Pochard/Ferruginous: I can't resist a note on this group as I remember it was the subject of endless confusion and discussion when I was a young birdwatcher and I dare say it still is! First, let's get one thing straight – Tufted and Pochard are the common ones. Scaup are pretty scarce inland, and local round the coasts mainly in winter. Real Ferruginous Ducks are a great rarity (though unfortunately there's a fair number of escapes at large). So inland reservoir watchers, as I was, live in hope of spotting a Scaup or better still a Ferruginous, and I well remember from my teen birding days how every week or so there'd be a report of a 'possible' Scaup or Ferruginous. In fact during over 10 years birding in the West Midlands I saw only 4 undeniable Scaup and 3 Ferruginous (only one of which I honestly considered a wild bird). The main culprits are juvenile and female Tufted Duck which can show a lot of white round the bill (like a female Scaup), or white under the tail (like a Ferruginous) and can vary in colour from washed out biscuit to rich tawny (like Scaup and Ferruginous respectively).

After 10 years of 'trying' with these birds I came to the correct conclusions which are:

- Female Scaup is bulkier than Tufted. Never shows even a vestige of a tuft on the back of its head and generally has a really good big white patch round its bill. It is also, more or less exclusively, only likely to be seen inland in winter.
- Ferruginous Duck females show no white on their faces, also have no tuft, have a head shape like a Pochard and are indeed a very pleasant Ferruginous colour

Where do Pochards come into this? Well, both male and female are not too hard to identify but they do have a naughty habit of cross-breeding with Tufteds and producing hybrids that can look rather like Ferruginous Ducks *or* Scaup (especially the exceptionally rare Lesser Scaup).

To sum up, I think I'd quote the rule I mentioned just before this section: 'If you're not sure . . . it isn't.' Or to put it another way: a 'funny Tufted' probably is . . . exactly that!

Yes, lot's of white on the face . . . and white undertail coverts . . . but it's still a Tufted.

SEA DUCKS: Eider, Long-tailed, Scoters and others

Another warning, but one to encourage the reservoir watcher. Sea ducks *are* obviously expected on the sea *but* they *do* occur inland now and again.

Eiders are the rarest inland and indeed they're not numerous around the coasts till you get up north near their breeding and main wintering grounds. To my mind they are the Gannet of the duck world! Nothing is easier than a male Eider in breeding plumage but the immatures go through all sorts of changes from black to white and various patterns in between. Fortunately the shape of an Eider is probably one of the most distinctive – so, faced with an Eider-shaped duck you might as well ask yourself 'what else could it be?' whatever the plumage. The only likely confusion I can think of is that a really dark one could look like a **scoter**, especially **Velvet Scoter** – so look out for the latter's white speculum.

Conversely, a stray Velvet Scoter could be mistaken for an Eider especially inland where you'd be expecting neither. **Common Scoters** do occur surprisingly often on reservoirs, sometimes in small parties. The males are easy but the females share white-ish faces with **Ruddy Duck**, **brownhead Smews** and some plumages of **Long-tailed Duck**.

The odd **Long-tailed Duck** which occasionally delights the reservoir watcher can be a bit of a puzzle. For a start, it won't have a long tail and the immatures have a very blotchy look about them that can remind you of a female **Pochard**, **Ruddy Duck** or **Common Scoter**. Generally, I think it more likely you could mistake a dowdy Long-tailed Duck for a commoner species rather than the other way round. In other words it's easily over-looked, especially as they seem to spend so much time under the water!

The same could be said of female **Goldeneyes** but certainly not of a drake **Smew**, perhaps *the* most exquisite of all ducks. The 'brownhead'

Long-tailed Duck and Porpoise or Loch Ness Monster . . . or diving Cormorant?

females, though, are less obvious and, as I said, could be mistaken for a small winter plumage grebe.

Finally **Red-breasted Mergansers** and **Goosanders** are big birds and the males superbly distinctive. Females, however, seen across choppy waters could resemble **Great Crested Grebes, Cormorants** or even **divers**. As regards distinguishing the two species, apart from plumage differences, a fair guideline is: Goosanders on inland waters and Mergansers on the sea and estuaries . . . though look out for the exceptions that prove the rule!

All in all then . . . a lot of thoughts about wildfowl but in the last analysis I really don't think it's a difficult group of birds . . . I wish I could say the same for the next lot!

BIRDS OF PREY (or, to use the more scientific term, Raptors)

Most birdwatchers, however experienced, would probably agree that this is the most difficult family of birds to identify. Fortunately, there are several excellent books to help us (see Book list, page 190) but the truth is there are some individual raptors that puzzle even the experts; and they wrote the books! So, why *are* raptors *so* difficult? Well I think for a start most birdwatchers simply don't see all that many of them – apart perhaps from Kestrels – so it's hard to get your eye in.

Secondly, they are very often way up in the sky either circling or flying away and their colours and plumage patterns don't show up very well. This means that we are relying very much on recognizing shapes and jizz and as we've already agreed, that takes practice. Add to this the fact that within various types of raptors the shapes are basically very similar – for example all falcons look basically the same, all harriers, eagles and so on. There *are* differences but they are subtle and it's rare that we see more than one species at a time so it's not often we can make direct comparisons. Finally, some species vary quite a bit in plumage – for example, Buzzards can look anything from almost black to almost white. Again this means that shape and size are all important.

As I said, there are some brilliant books available so obviously I recommend them highly. I'd also suggest a few rules to help your raptor-watching.

First, don't panic! Raptors do have a habit of circling up so high you'll lose sight of them or dashing over the horizon never to appear again – so if you do see one keep your eyes on it as long as possible before it vanishes! Don't start writing notes whilst the bird is still visible unless it's clearly going to be around for a while. Then, try and get a good description of the underside pattern when the bird is flying overhead, as this is often the most crucial feature. Raptors perched are, funnily enough, often harder to identify than when they are flying. However, if you see one in a tree or on a post and you're not sure what it is, *don't* immediately walk closer to get it to take off. It probably will, but it's likely to zoom out of sight completely. Have patience and with luck it'll fly off in a more leisurely fashion and even circle overhead. Perhaps more than with any other group it's worth bearing in mind the *likelihood* of any particular species being seen where and when you happen to be, and definitely assume it is the *most* likely bird you're looking at until proved otherwise. For example in mountainous or hilly regions a large bird of prey is most likely to be a Common Buzzard, especially if it's summertime. On the other hand, if it's midwinter on the flat coast of Norfolk or North Kent then a buzzard-like raptor is more likely to be the scarce Rough-legged Buzzard. (Always assuming you've discounted harriers and Short-eared Owls – which we'll come to in a minute!) I'll say it again – don't panic. Study the books and ask the experts if they are on hand – and be encouraged rather than disappointed if occasionally they admit they're not sure what it was either! A couple of other tips for spotting birds of prey in the first place: first watch out for excitable behaviour from other birds. If you're on a marsh and suddenly all the gulls and wildfowl take flight for no apparent reason, scan the skies and nearby horizon – chances are there's a Marsh Harrier or a Peregrine around, or even an Osprey overhead. Smaller birds may well be mobbing a Merlin or Kestrel in the same kind of area. The same applies in woodlands: sudden squeaking and scolding from small birds may well lead you to a raptor trying to take a quiet nap in a tree, and eventually they may chase it out and help you identify it.

Second tip: if it's a warm day look out for birds circling on the thermals. Beware though as it's by no means just raptors that do this – gulls do it a lot and can certainly be mistaken for raptors. On the other hand if there are gulls up there . . . a bird of prey may join them. On days like that it's worth looking up every ten minutes or so to see if anything new has floated into the spiral. Once birds are circling they may be in view for quite a time in more or less the same place. Long enough even to train a telescope on them – it's a skill worth practising. They may also get very high indeed and you may not always spot them with the naked eye, so . . . use your binoculars to scan around.

One last warning – when looking for larger raptors you'll soon learn to curse Crows (and Rooks and Ravens). They do very good impressions of birds of prey as they circle in the thermals, flap lazily over the hilltops, or even glide as if pursuing prey. Still, if you're looking for any particular raptor please *don't* be afraid to yell: 'Is that it?' – no-one will really blame you if it turns out to be 'only a crow', and next time it won't be. This is particularly likely to happen when you're looking for . . .

BUZZARDS, EAGLES AND LARGER RAPTORS

Everyone *wants* to see an eagle and it's amazing how many people do. It's especially amazing when they tell me they've seen them on holiday in Devon or South Wales – the people I mean, not the eagles. The fact is eagles don't go on holiday or anything else to Devon or South Wales. There *is* a pair of Golden Eagles in the Lake District, so well protected by wardens that you'll either not see them at all or share the experience with a small crowd. Otherwise Golden Eagles *only* occur in Scotland and the Western Isles. A small number of White-tailed (Sea) Eagles have been introduced to the same area in recent years and have even successfully bred. So, it's only way up north that you are likely to see an Eagle. Even up there they are not numerous, and the chances are still overwhelming that a large bird of prey will be a Buzzard. Buzzards can look very big but believe me eagles are massive. The old rule applies again: 'If you're not sure . . . it isn't'. When you *do* see an eagle you'll know. Golden Eagles in flight look as huge as vultures – Sea Eagles look like barn doors!

All the other species of large raptors – let's say roughly buzzard-sized – are either scarce or localized in their habits and habitats: Red Kites restricted to certain parts of Wales, Marsh Harriers in Eastern England and so on. So check those distribution maps in the field guide and think twice if you see them away from expected areas. One bird that is delightfully unpredictable on spring passage is the superb Osprey which certainly can and has dropped in for a quick fish supper at virtually any inland reservoir as well as its more favoured stopovers. And, by the way, there are now *several* pairs breeding in Scotland so you don't necessarily *have* to be in a hide at Loch Garten to see one!

What are the other confusion species for these large raptors? We've already mentioned airborne gulls and crows. Short-eared Owls and sometimes Long-eareds hunt during daylight hours and quarter the fields in a similar style to harriers and could definitely be mistaken for the browner females. Mind you, technically owls are also birds of prey so they *ought* to be confusable!

Male harriers are pretty distinctive but I did hear a report of a male **Montagu's Harrier** supposedly regularly roosting at dusk on the roof of a harbour-side church on the Isles of Scilly. I checked it out and found – an adult **Herring Gull!** Now that may seem pretty daft, but if you think about it: a Herring Gull gliding in through the gloom . . . a big long winged grey bird with black wing tips . . . much the same description as a male harrier! Not that I've *ever* heard of a real harrier roosting on a church roof! Oh, before we leave the big ones, one last warning for the rarity hunters – if you think you've been lucky enough to see a **Black Kite,** are you absolutely certain it wasn't a female Marsh Harrier? *Very* similar jizz those two, especially floating away on a hot hazy day when there's nothing much else around to get excited about. . . . Oh – you definitely saw the forked tail . . . wish *I'd* been there!

THE SMALLER ONES
Sparrowhawk and Kestrel

A question I'm asked a lot is: 'We've got a small bird of prey that perches on the roof near our flats – is it a Kestrel or a Sparrowhawk?' Well, I don't even have to see that bird to be 99.9% certain – it's a Kestrel. A pretty safe rule this one: Sparrowhawks live and hunt in woodlands where they hunt by flying low alongside and through the trees. They *never* hover and they rarely come into towns and I've never yet seen one perched on a building or telegraph wires (though I suppose they *could* if they tried)!

Kestrels live both in towns and in woods. They do hover and they perch just about anywhere. So, if the bird's flying through woods it could be either: but if it's hovering over the motorway, or perching on wires or poles, or living in town – you can bet it's a Kestrel. In fact, if you see them well, their plumages are quite different. The Sparrowhawk is barred underneath and looks, flies like, and is often mistaken for a Cuckoo.

Falcons: Kestrel, Merlin, Hobby and Peregrine

I said before that all falcons are *basically* a similar shape – sleek, sharp winged, fast flyers – and it's true. Just look at a page-full in the field guide. They're not impossible though and again there are vital clues in where and when you see them. For example, Hobbies are only summer visitors and only breed in the southern half of England, Merlins belong more up north on the moorlands, whilst Peregrines favour cliffs and mountain regions – though both Merlins and Peregrines come down to the coastal areas outside the breeding season. Kestrels occur everywhere!

Circling Raptors – or are they? After all, the bird on p. 67 was only a Crow!

So, again, check those maps and habitats carefully . . . but a general warning when you think you've spotted a fast moving falcon: beware of **pigeons!**

Pigeons and **doves** – whether wild or domestic – can race around the skies in a manner that is very like a falcon. A big grey pigeon especially can do a terrific impression of a Peregrine as it dives into the cliffs. The one consolation is it may well be being chased *by* a Peregrine so you may get the chance to compare the two! Woodpigeons even have a soaring display-flight that is very reminiscent of a bird of prey lunging over the tree tops.

So . . . to sum up. Birds of prey often give us tantalizingly awkward views and at such times they are often difficult to identify. Moreover, when seen equally briefly or at a distance, there are several confusion species – herons, gulls, crows, owls, cuckoos and pigeons. On the other hand, raptors may be perplexing but they are also brilliant! When you do see them well . . . it's an unforgettable experience.

GAME-BIRDS

Generally you shouldn't have too much trouble with **grouse**, **pheasants** and **partridges** except where there are wandering **chickens** and **guinea fowl** around (and there are even a few escaped **peacocks** roaming the English countryside and the dull brown females – peahens – do look rather like giant pheasants!). When distinguishing between real game birds remember the rules of habitat and geography. **Ptarmigan** and **Capercaillies** *only* live in Scotland; **Black** and **Red Grouse** only on or close by moorlands; **Red-legged Partridges** are absent from most of western and northern Britain and so on. Game-birds are often hard to get a good view of as they scurry through the heather or crops, so these kind of distributional clues really do help. For example, if you see even a tantalizing glimpse of a partridge in Ireland – it's *not* Red-legged – they don't occur there. When looking for partridges scan the fields with binoculars, but don't be fooled by feeding pigeons.

Also beware of misidentifying birds that are not yet fully grown but *are* fully mobile. Many an infant Pheasant or partridge has been called a **Quail** as it scampers into a barley field. Quails are very scarce and more often heard than seen. Similarly teenage-equivalent Pheasants can look like partridges and young Capercailies look more like grouse. It's not a problem that exists outside a month or two in summer and early autumn – they soon grow up!

There are also a number of exotic pheasants that have established themselves in the wild in Britain. Two of them are now more or less accepted as honorary British citizens, **Golden Pheasant** and **Lady Amherst's,** and there are others that must be on the brink.

All of them – or at least the males – are dazzling looking birds and well worth seeing. They may hybridize with Common Pheasants which are slightly variable in plumage anyway. No pheasants migrate so I suppose a sobering rule if you ever see a funny pheasant is don't get too excited – it *can't* be a genuine rarity! (Unless of course it's a **bustard** in which case, you've *really* hit the jackpot. You shouldn't even *think* about seeing bustards but if you want to check them out have a glance at the rarities pages in the field guide.)

A Quail? . . . Or is it a young something or other?

RAILS AND CRAKES (including Moorhen and Coot)

It's a pretty good rule for bird identification to say, 'start from what you know'. Moorhens and Coots are pretty familiar birds and indeed the adults are easy to recognize. Telling them apart tends to be one of the first lessons for novice birdwatchers. 'Coots are the black ones with white beaks yes?' – Yes. 'Bald as a coot', that's supposed to be the white bit over the beak. However, it's the young birds that can cause confusion.

Young Moorhens are pretty dull creatures and they remain so through much of their first winter. They are easily mistaken for Water Rails – which are difficult to see but not incredibly rare – or the genuinely rare crakes (Spotted, Little and Baillon's) – which *are* pretty rare! So, simple rule, before claiming a rare crake: be sure it's not a young moorhen or just a Water Rail.

Juvenile Coots are, rather surprisingly, white underneath and as I've already suggested do look a bit like Black-necked or Slavonian Grebes in winter plumage.

Another statement of the obvious. Coots can fly. Actually though, we don't often see them at it! So, it's rather like with Great Crested Grebes, a flying Coot can be a momentary puzzle – especially if it's quite well up above the water . . . is it a duck? . . . a scoter? . . . no . . . just a Coot.

Lastly in this group, the Corncrake is sadly now restricted to Western Scotland, the Western Isles and Ireland. If you think you've seen one anywhere else – think again!

WADERS

I have come across birdwatchers who have terrible trouble with waders, especially in America. I remember visiting a bird reserve near New York and asking a local to help me sort out the small 'peeps' which is what Americans call mud-feeding stints and sandpipers. 'Don't ask me,' came the reply, 'I don't bother with peeps. They all look the same to me.' Well the truth is, *some* of them *do* look the same, or very similar, but none of them are unidentifiable, and since there's nothing bird experts like more than a challenge there are now some brilliant pages of illustrations in the latest field guides and some wonderful books devoted to wader identification (see page 190). Moreover, unlike raptors, waders are not difficult birds to observe. In fact they are usually amongst the easiest. Almost inevitably a new birdwatcher's first trip away from his or her home-patch will be to a reserve such as Minsmere, Cley, or Blacktoft and one of the chief attractions will be the waders. Unlike birds of prey, they tend to potter around on mud, or marshy ground and allow you to study them, with a telescope even, and compare different species and their respective plumages, feeding styles and jizzes. Within the whole group of waders there is wondrous variety – including such totally unmistakable birds as **Lapwings**, and **Oystercatchers**. In fact, if waders do frighten you a little, may I start off by suggesting you flick through the field guide ticking off the ones you *do* know. You'll be pleasantly surprised. Then there'll be other little groups or pairs you can be sure of: it's either a **Ringed Plover**, **Little Ringed Plover**, or **Kentish Plover** . . . or it's a godwit not sure which one but it *is* a godwit . . . or it's a **Curlew** or **Whimbrel** . . . or **Green** or **Wood Sandpiper**. I'm willing to bet by the time you've calmly been through them all you'll come to the conclusion that there's actually only a handful that *really* puzzle you. The secret is this process of elimination. Faced with a wader you don't immediately recognize – rapidly go through what it *isn't* and you'll be down to a small number of choices very quickly. Then you can *really* concentrate and *enjoy* sorting it out.

Another encouraging fact: there are very few non-waders that can confuse the issue. In flight small flocks of **pigeons** (what else!?) can look similar to a flock of middle sized waders – but generally speaking a wader is easily recognized as just that, especially once it's wading.

Mind you, having said that, there are several species that are frequently seen on and actually prefer short grassy areas like golf courses, aerodromes or low cropped fields. They still look like waders though.

So – it's pretty easy to spot a wader, and pretty easy to narrow it down to a handful of species. But once you've done that – what next? OK, I'll own up, it *can* be quite difficult . . . but it's *great* fun.

One thing to remember above all: the plumage of most (but not all) waders changes quite a bit throughout the year. Full summer or breeding plumages are generally easy to recognize but winter and juvenile plumages are much less distinctive. The best field guides show them all.

Second piece of advice: *listen*. The calls of waders are almost without exception 'diagnostic': which means if it calls you should eventually be able to put a name to it. Distinguishing between calls obviously takes practice and experience but it's not too difficult to gain. Most waders are noisy birds, especially when they first take off. So if you're watching a wader, even if you recognize it by sight make a point of trying to hear its call. Once you know the commonest calls you'll immediately be aware of an uncommon call. Many rare waders have been discovered this way. I remember birdwatching in southern Ireland one September. It was a marshland near the sea shore. The tide was coming up and covering the beach and waders were flying everywhere looking for roosting places. The air was full of calls: Ringed Plovers and Dunlin, Turnstone and Sanderling, Curlews, Oystercatchers, Grey and Golden Plovers. It was quite a cacophony but I *knew* all the various sounds – except one. A plaintive whistle that sounded like something between a Grey and a Golden Plover. I didn't know what it was but I knew I'd never heard it before. For what seemed like half an hour – but was probably half a minute – I scanned the clouds above till I spotted the bird. In silhouette it indeed looked like a Golden Plover and yet slightly slimmer and longer winged . . . more like a Ruff perhaps. But I knew what noise Ruffs make – usually none at all! and if they do it's a soft 'chuck'. I tried to imitate the call. The bird circled over me, and whether it was impressed or irritated by my impersonation I don't know, but it pitched on to the shingle only twenty yards away. I was pretty sure what it was, and two pages of field notes and a look through the field guide confirmed it: my first American Lesser Golden Plover (at that time only about the third or fourth recorded in Ireland I think).

Sorry about the digression – happy memories – but I hope it makes a point. Get to know your wader calls and even have a go yourself!

American Golden Plover about to touch down in Ireland. Think of it . . . it's just crossed the Atlantic, and probably non-stop.

So, I'm sending you back to the books, the tapes and records and of course, the birds. I will though just add a quick miscellany of 'wader confusions I have known' . . .

PLOVERS: Ringed, Little Ringed and Kentish

Adults aren't too bad if you get a good view but juveniles are notorious. Always remember that **Ringed Plover** is the commonest. **Little Ringed Plover** is the next most likely and **Kentish** is pretty rare. So if you *think* you *might* have a Kentish you probably haven't. I don't mean this to be as glib as it sounds.

For fifteen years or more I'd get excited by any number of 'possible' Kentish Plovers. Then one September on a Suffolk beach at the ripe old age of twenty six I saw my first Kentish Plover. At that moment all those 'possibles' identified themselves once and for all as young Ringed Plovers with breast bands that didn't meet. They *did* look very like Kentish Plovers, if I overlooked the fact that their legs weren't black – but they just *weren't*. Why? The jizz was wrong. It's that rarity rule again: 'If you're not sure . . . it probably isn't.' It has a second part, and Kentish Plover is an excellent example: 'When you see one – you know.'

It's a good rule for a lot of waders.

Oh, I can't leave Ringed Plovers without mentioning my favourite misidentification (though it wasn't by me . . . honestly). A report of an Alpine Swift – which turned out to be a Ringed Plover doing its display flight. Again there's logic in it: the plover has a breast band and does zoom around on oddly stiff wings. By and large though Alpine Swifts don't run around on beaches and stick their beaks into mud – or if they do they're in dead trouble.

Talking of display flights – Golden Plover have a weird soaring flight. I recall seeing one looming out of the mountain mists somewhere on Shetland and misidentifying it as a small raptor. See – we all make silly mistakes.

I had contemplated going through *all* the waders since, as you may have gathered, it's one of my favourite groups and I could go on and on but I mustn't, not least because other books have already done it, and much better too with wonderful illustrations. But just a few more random tips: get to know your habitats – or rather particular waders' habitats, which are usually related to their feeding preferences. Which

Waders against the light ... a good chance to study jizz ... but so much nicer if you move where the sun's behind you.

species prefer freshwater pools, and which favour seaside estuaries, or beaches; and which like shingle or rocks or short grass? It'll all help you know where to look and what to expect.

Check those tide tables and find the places where the birds roost or congregate as the water is coming up or receding. (See Estuaries, page 77.) Don't panic about 'peeps'. Study the commonest species, particularly Dunlin. It's amazing how many reported rarities turn out to be 'funny Dunlin'. Practise comparing all other small waders with Dunlin – size, shape, bill length, feeding style and movements and so on.

And, as ever, don't be afraid to make mistakes. If it'll make you feel better, I'll finish with a couple more of my own. I once reported a summer plumage Grey Phalarope on Cley Marshes that I know perfectly well was in fact a summer plumaged Knot – both are red underneath with short straight beaks! Then, to make it worse, a week later I saw a *winter* plumage Grey Phalarope flying past when I was sea-watching that then landed on the beach and turned into a Sanderling. Later the same year I recorded yet another Grey Phalarope on a small pond just up the coast and – surprise surprise – nobody believed me. But it *was*! Ah well ... that's how we learn these things.

SKUAS

If you're lucky enough to visit the breeding colonies of **Great** or **Arctic Skuas** up in Shetland you certainly won't have much trouble identifying them: and they'll soon identify you too and dive-bomb to prove it –

they're not keen on intruders wandering through the colony. Otherwise, spotting a skua is another perk of sea-watching, which means that chances are it'll be a relatively distant speck way out towards the horizon and mixed up with all those confusable young **Gannets**, and worse still, **young gulls.** Juvenile Herring and also Lesser Black-backs can look very dark, especially against the light, and they do sometimes even behave like skuas, chasing smaller gulls or terns. Once you've seen a few real skuas though you'll soon begin to appreciate their distinctive style of flying and harassing other birds. 'Bonxies' (Great Skuas) aren't difficult to identify out at sea but distinguishing between the others – Arctic, Pomarine and Long-tailed is quite a tricky business when young birds are involved. Remember the likelihood factor: Arctics are by far the commonest, then 'Poms' – especially on the south coasts in spring when they sometimes pass in quite sizable parties – and Long-tails are definitely rare. So to be safe assume Arctic till proved otherwise!

GULLS

A much neglected group although perhaps becoming less so in recent years. Even birdwatchers tend to dismiss everything as 'sea-gulls' when in fact there's quite a number of different common species in the country and often in the same flock. Mind you, that may be one of the problems – gulls do gather in *huge* flocks especially at their roosts, and sorting through them searching for a potential rarity can be quite a daunting business. It's worth it though, as gull watchers have discovered all sorts of exciting birds. It was only a few years ago that Britain's first American Ring-billed Gull was spotted by keen eyes amongst thousands of Common Gulls in South Wales. It's now recorded regularly round the country – sometimes more than 100 in a year, and that's probably due to sharper watching rather than more birds.

I really do recommend sorting through gull flocks. Set up a telescope and just pan slowly through them. You'll be encouraged by how quickly you're able to dismiss the commoner species even though they do come in a bewildering range of plumages. Then just now and then you'll see a 'funny gull' that isn't just in some strange moult – it's a real rarity. It happened to me in Hampshire a few years ago, and in mid-July too, which was particularly strange since it's often assumed *that* rare gulls only occur in the more wintry months. In this case, I was using gull-scanning as an excuse for a rest after tramping round Farlington Marshes on a hot day. I worked my way through at least a couple of hundred

Black-headed Gulls, adults, juveniles and some in between when I arrived at a slightly smaller bird. A Little Gull? No, not quite that small, and it didn't look right for a Little Gull either. In fact it looked more like a small Black-headed Gull. Maybe it *was* just a runt Black-headed, such things could happen, but no, it flapped as it splashed and preened and revealed a clear white wedge on its underwing flight feathers. This, and other minute details, confirmed it as a Bonaparte's Gull – a very rare visitor from America. Bonaparte's Gulls are usually identified somewhere down in Cornwall in midwinter (and then no more than one or two a year) . . . but where do these strays go in summer? Well this one was apparently moulting with its British cousins in Hampshire. Maybe more rare winter gulls do that. But they're not found because nobody looks! So . . . as I said, *do* scan through the gulls. Rarities can occur inland too – so try reservoirs and rubbish tips as well as coastal roosts. And even if you don't find anything – it's a great excuse for a sit down!

Black-headed Gulls in three plumages, plus a sleepy Bonaparte's.

Gull identification requires experience and a good eye. Again there are excellent books available. I will refer to one classic confusion though – juvenile **Kittiwakes** which are pretty common on sea-watches are *always* being misreported as **Sabine's Gulls** (another rarity from across the Atlantic). Well it's very much the same sort of principle as Ringed and Kentish Plovers. I went for years and years staring over the ocean waves hoping to see a Sabine's Gull and indeed seeing several birds I thought *might* have been. Funnily enough though they were always far out to sea, usually flying away from me. It's a fact really – the *further* a juvenile Kittiwake is away the *more* it looks like a Sabine's Gull! The truth is of course that if it were any closer you wouldn't get so excited – you'd see it was 'only a Kittiwake'. As it happened though my first real Sabine's was also way off over the horizon, and to make it more difficult I was bobbing up and down in a boat at the time. And yet I recognized it immediately.

Why? Well, it was the way it flew, the style . . . the jizz . . . it just *wasn't* like a Kittiwake. More like a Little Gull perhaps? Well, a bit . . . a tern-like flight maybe? Yes, in a way . . . but most of all it looked like . . . well, a Sabine's Gull. 'When you see one – you know.' And just to make sure I'd seen this one properly it flew closer and closer and ended up eating fish scraps at the back of the boat.

Juvenile Kittiwakes and a 'probable' Sabine's Gull. If it was moving, it'd be a 'definite'!

By and large, gulls are gulls – some of the smaller ones do have rather tern-like flights but I think only Little Gulls could momentarily be confused with real terns. On the other hand, distant flights of large gulls can look very like big **waders** – Curlews for example – and when they fly in a V they could even be mistaken for **geese**. Also, as I've already warned don't be fooled by **raptor-impersonators** circling on the thermals.

A last word in praise of gulls. If you ever end up doing a 24-hour bird race it's always encouraging to think that with any luck at all you've got at least five easy ticks for a kick off – all gulls.

Five easy ticks!

TERNS: The white ones
COMMON, ARCTIC, ROSEATE, LITTLE, SANDWICH

Not a lot of problem deciding a tern is a tern (as long as it isn't a Little Gull). Some are pretty easy to identify, some less so . . . and out on a sea-watch all can be a bit tricky till you get your eye in. One nice recent development is the increasing number of Common Terns breeding inland – I've even got a few pairs just up the road from me that nest on artificial platforms on a London Reservoir, and even come fishing on my local duckponds on Hampstead Heath.

Marsh Terns: *BLACK TERNS*

A nice flock of summer plumage **Black Terns** – look for them in May after east winds both on the coast and over inland waters – are not only a delight but also pretty unmistakable. In autumn plumages though they can be puzzlers. I have a page from my very first big notebook from September in Norfolk where I record 'an unfamiliar bird seen flying a few hundred yards out to sea which looked grey on top and white below and had an almost square tail.' It flew steadily and didn't glide, and I had no idea what it was. At first I entertained thoughts of a 'first for Britain' but the fact that I saw three or four more the next day eventually persuaded me it was probably something relatively common. Eventually I realized I was looking at Black Terns – it was not a new bird for me but previously I'd only seen them in spring swooping and hawking over a Midlands reservoir looking as black as Black Terns surely should. It was a valuable double lesson:

(a) that some birds' plumage changes dramatically during the year and
(b) that a familiar bird in an unfamiliar setting can completely throw you (well it threw *me* anyway, so I just thought I'd mention it in case it ever happens to you).

Also – as I suggested before – if your Black Tern is in November and way out over the water . . . and especially if it seems to have a more or less white rump . . . are you sure it's not a **Leach's Petrel**? and if it is, well done!

AUKS: Razorbills, Guillemots and Puffins

Another group that's easy on the cliffs and a bit of a headache when they're racing past out at sea. The safe way out is simply to record them all as 'auks sp.' – which means you're not sure which is which. If it's any consolation, a lot of pretty expert sea-watchers do just that. **Puffins** flying by do look smaller but the other two are very similar and it takes a *lot* of practice to separate them. Fortunately you're not really likely to mistake auks for anything else, though I have heard of at least one report of a **penguin** that I'm afraid I didn't really believe.

The odd one out here is the little Black Guillemot. In summer plumage no problem, but it's another one that fades to almost white in winter and goes through blotchy stages in between that make a distant bird bobbing on a rough sea look rather reminiscent of a **Long-tailed Duck** or even a **phalarope**. It's not at all numerous off southern coasts but odd ones do occur and since generally birdwatchers aren't really expecting them they can be puzzlers at first.

PIGEONS

A good rule of bird-watching which may sound a bit frivolous but isn't entirely so: if you're really puzzled by an odd looking bird – was it a **Domestic Pigeon**? There are lots of them around, all flying and behaving

And every one a pigeon!

as if they were perfectly wild and they come in all sorts of weird colours and quite a few shapes and sizes. Generally they're not a problem when they're not in the air, especially if they're feeding out of your hand, but I have known flying pigeons mistaken for all sorts of things from Peregrines, Hobbies and Gyrfalcons to Sandgrouse and White-winged Black Terns! This is partly because they are in the habit of appearing in silly places – I've seen one almost cause a twitch on the scrape at Minsmere and another one joining a flock of Manx Shearwaters a mile off the Pembroke Coast. So, a motto: be prepared for pigeons.

If you do mistake one for something don't be afraid to own up. It happens to us all. I simply do not believe that even the most experienced birdwatcher sometimes think he's seen a plummeting raptor, or a migrating flock of waders, or a pack of Teal when in his heart of hearts he knows they were really pigeons.

RING-NECKED PARAKEET

It seems rather ironical that in recent years I've been approached by embarrassed members of the public who say . . . 'er sorry to bother you, but I've seen a funny bird. It *looked* like some sort of parrot . . . but what was it *really?*' Well, it really *was* some sort of parrot! Ring-necked Parakeets are now free-flying in several parts of Britain and are no doubt

due to be given British passports if they survive a few more winters. So don't worry if you see one! Nice birds – though they do make a horrible noise.

CUCKOO

We've all heard 'em but how many have we seen? It's never easy, unless you're lucky enough to be led to one by a foster-parent feeding it, it's most likely you'll see a Cuckoo skimming low over fields or marshes or gliding into the woods looking very like a Sparrowhawk. Also, brown ones *do* occur – either in a rare colour phase (that are *really* brown) or juveniles that are more browny grey.

OWLS

Another group we hear more than see, though in fact they are visible rather more than non-birdwatchers realize. The **Short-eared Owl** is the most frequent daytime feeder when it quarters the coastal fields tempting us to misidentify it as a **female harrier. Long-eareds** on migration sometimes do the same. A white owl anywhere but Shetland is, of course, going to be a **Barn Owl** – not a **Snowy Owl** – and they quite often fly at dawn and dusk. **Little** and **Tawny Owls** are pretty much nocturnal but even they can be flushed out during the day and make short reluctant flights when, at a fleeting glimpse, they can pass for **hawks.** As I suggested with raptors you may often be led to a roosting owl by small birds mobbing it and in fact you may even get excellent views of the small birds too! The *only* time I've ever enjoyed a real close-up of the tiny **Scops Owl** was in Majorca. It sat resignedly and looking decidedly fed up in a tree no more than ten feet from me whilst a mixed pack of little birds scolded it and dared one another to flap in its face, giving me the chance not only to study the owl but also to compare at least half a dozen species of warblers.

KINGFISHER

Seems silly to even mention a bird so well known but . . . I recall as a very young birdwatcher being distinctly puzzled when a bright blue bird flashed by me as I walked by my local canal and, ten minutes later, a bright orange one flew back. It was another ten minutes before I realized it was the same bird, and that there are two sides to every Kingfisher!

NIGHTJAR

Another one I took years to see. They *are* very local and very elusive and you need to wait patiently in the right place and at the right time of day – or rather evening. Birdwatchers are pretty generous about letting one another know the 'sites' of good birds and I really do suggest if you want to see a Nightjar it's worth checking out the places they are known to be present. If you're well informed and you get lucky you'll see it flitting around in the dusk like a ghostly falcon. I always feel strangely privileged to see one at all. Once you've accepted just how scarce they are it's not likely you'll come up with any faulty sightings . . . or hearings. I have known some though. Nightjars, according to the books, make a loud 'churring' sound not unlike the engine of a small motor scooter, and I've certainly known over-optimistic Nightjar hunters be fooled by just that . . . distant *motor scooters, generators, frogs, crickets,* and indeed other Nightjar hunters playing *tapes!*

Visually, I'd always thought a Nightjar was pretty unmistakeable until very recently a neighbour called me to say that he'd got a Nightjar in his garden. This, in North London in December, was extremely unlikely – they're summer migrants and they don't live in this area. Nevertheless, he went on to give a pretty convincing description: 'It sits along a large branch; it's rather an elongated bird, sort of scaly brown on top, I think it's got a bit of white on the edge of its tail, and it's got this rattling call.' I went to see it . . . and found . . . a **Mistle Thrush**! Just goes to show how wrong good descriptions can be!

HOOPOE

I have to mention it as I think it must be *the* bird every birdwatcher wants to see. It doesn't seem fair then that they seem to be seen more often by holidaymakers in Spain, or vicars who've been blessed by a rare migrant feeding on their lawn in Suffolk. If you *do* see one, they're terrific – in flight they look like a great big black-and-white butterfly and on the ground a bit like a cross between a Jay and a small zebra! So in theory I suppose a Jay ought to be a confusion species but it isn't really.

WRYNECK

A rare bird that looks like a small woodpecker in Nightjar's clothing. If you see one it's likely to be in May or August/September and probably on

the east coast when there are lots of other scarce migrants around and lots of other birdwatchers to confirm what it is. One little warning though – it may indeed be related to woodpeckers *but* on migration it's likely to be hopping along a drystone wall or feeding on the ground. . . .

WOODPECKERS: Greater Spotted, Lesser Spotted and Green

The Wryneck's not the only one! **Green Woodpeckers** often feed on the ground too, and then they flit ahead and away showing only a bright yellow rump. There is no doubt that many dodgy reports of **Golden Orioles** are in fact Green Woodpeckers (see Golden Oriole, later). I'm sure it's partly because you don't really *expect* a woodpecker to be on the ground and so it's not the species that first springs to mind when this big lemon-rumped bird flips tantalizingly away looking ever so exotic. Nevertheless, it is most probably a Green Woodpecker.

The two Spotteds more often stick to the woods where they belong except **Great Spotteds** do come to garden feeders and are a constant source of puzzlement to non-birdwatchers. 'I've got this escaped bird in my garden . . . big as a Starling . . . bright red head'. . . . Great Spotted, definitely.

OK – HALF TIME

Funnily enough there's a sort of natural break here. So far we've been dealing largely with birds that are fairly big and often quite distinctively coloured. They have their problems – or rather birdwatchers have *their* problems – but just in case you're feeling remotely bewildered by it all, please please don't. By and large, the majority of birds so far are really not that hard to identify . . . well, not compared with the *next* lot anyway. No . . . sorry . . . only joking. . . .

Nevertheless, we now come to what are sometimes referred to as the 'little brown jobs' (not to be confused with what puppies do on carpets). In fact they are by no means *all* brown – and they're not *all* little – but *some* of them are and they are a wondrous challenge to birdwatchers, beginners and experts alike. Nevertheless – I've said it before and I'll say it again – *that's* what makes it fun! I hope you enjoy sorting them out as much as I do.

Before we start on them, may I just re-iterate those basic rules. Always be thinking 'what do I expect to see?' in any particular habitat. 'What is *likely* to be here?' Take your notes – literally or mentally. Look at the beak, the way it moves, what it's feeding on and ask yourself what *family* does this bird look as though it belongs to? Take note of any obvious plumage features. If there *don't* seem to be any – if it really *does* look like a little brown job – check the key areas, like the face pattern, the rump, the tail, the breast and so on. . . .

Listen – does it make any noises?

And try the process of elimination approach – what *isn't* it?

As before, the following pages are tips and friendly warnings about common confusions – I hope they help. Good luck. . . . Oh and if you want an incentive . . . just imagine next time you're out with a couple of friends and you see some dowdy little warblery thing dive into a gorse bush and one of them asks: 'What was *that*?' . . . and the other one says: 'Don't ask me, some little brown job' . . . but you say: 'Female White-throat' . . . Boy, will they be impressed, and you'll feel *great*! (I just hope you were right!)

LARKS AND PIPITS

'Roughly sparrow-sized, streaky crown on top, whitish underneath but with streaks on the breast, white in the outer tail feathers, spends a lot of time on the ground.' Feed that one into the computer and it'd come up with a selection of larks, pipits . . . and female buntings. Fair enough too.

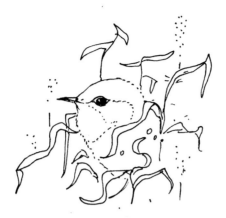

Oh, yes . . . you were right. It was a Whitethroat

In fact larks and pipits are closely related and you'll find them pretty close to each other – and easily compared – in the field guides. The buntings though are right at the end. So are female buntings genuine confusion species for larks and pipits? Generally I'd say 'not really'. So that's good news isn't it!? Certainly it won't be a problem if you get a decent look at the beaks. Pipits have fine narrow little beaks, larks are a little thicker, but buntings are stubby (real seed-eating beaks). However, remember these notes are concerned with birds we *don't* see all that well. It's true that pipits, larks and buntings *do* all spend a lot of time scuffling around on the ground in stubble fields and short grass, so often all that one sees of them is mainly their backs, not their beaks. You'll get an immediate clue by the *way* they move. Pipits walk and run, larks shuffle and then run, and buntings, in most cases, just shuffle and hop. The only real confusion occurs with the one bunting that really can run: the scarce **Lapland Bunting**, which both in jizz and movement could truly be said to be 'lark-like'. Fortunately – or unfortunately perhaps – 'Laps' are rare birds and only likely to be found in small parties in some coastal regions in autumn or winter.

This lark/bunting similarity is not one usually referred to in the books. I do hope it's not just a personal problem *I* have! Things are difficult enough without adding confusions which don't worry most people. But it *has* happened to me – twice. I recall a single Lapland Bunting in dowdy female plumage leading me (*and* a friend, so it wasn't *just* me) a right old chase across the tiny island of Out Skerries in Shetland. It was late May and neither of us were expecting Lapland Buntings, but we *were*

A Lark or a Bunting?

rather hoping for some rare lark. The skulking brown job that kept flitting on 100 yards ahead of us seemed a likely candidate. Only after half an hour did a third friend join us. He was not perhaps as experienced as we were supposed to be. He took one look at the bird and asked: 'Why isn't it a Lapland Bunting?' It was a good question, because that's exactly what it was. Our companion hadn't even *heard* of the rare larks we were trying to turn it into! You see, too much knowledge can be a dangerous thing. I also recall an autumn on Fair Isle when there was a single Short-toed Lark (another rare one – don't try looking for the short toes!) and a single Lapland Bunting frequenting the same stubble fields: I know they were often mistaken for one another in flight (because I did it myself). Furthermore, several times I've flushed what I at first assumed was a female bunting from a coastal meadow only to watch it land and reveal itself to be a Tree Pipit. So I reckon there must be *something* in it. Not only do all these birds share roughly the same plumage but there must be at least some small similarities of jizz in certain views.

Having said all that, please don't worry too much about it. Most of the time buntings look like buntings (see Buntings, page 167). Larks and pipits do sometimes take a bit of separating. The first thing to remember is that Skylarks don't always show great big crests and they certainly aren't always singing their heads off way up in the sky. In autumn and winter they gather in feeding flocks that may be seen virtually anywhere from farmland to the sea shore, and at such times they often make an odd squeaky call (rarely mentioned in the books) that is quite different from the familiar 'chirrup'. A single bird making this call could be a bit of a puzzle at first. Or if it makes no noise at all . . . another confession coming up. My first big notebook – as well as containing the Black Tern error – also has an account of a 'possible Richard's Pipit' I saw on

Dawlish Warren in Devon in September 1955 when I was 14 (OK, go on work it out). It's a good rare bird spot and a good rare bird time of the year and when I saw what I took to be a large pipit scurrying through the tussocky grass I also remembered reading in some book that that was exactly the right kind of habitat for the rare large pipits: Richard's and Tawny. This bird was very streaky above and below so it *had* to be a Richard's. (If you're not familiar with the species have a look at the book and you'll see it's not an entirely silly conclusion). However, to my eternal shame I managed to ignore the fact that later on in the day I saw a small party of birds that looked *very* similar that I instantly recognized as Skylarks. Nevertheless, so anxious was I to see a rarity that I purposely *didn't* go back to refind that single bird and make absolutely certain it didn't have the teeniest quiff of a crest or make a noise I'd have to admit was definitely Skylarky. At least I had a sufficient sense of guilt to never send in the record and I only ticked it in pencil on my checklist. Four or five years later I saw my first Richard's Pipit in late September in Shetland: it was in a similar kind of habitat and it was indeed brown and streaky above with streaks on the breast, white outer tail etc . . . and I even wrote – 'about the same size as a Skylark' – but it didn't really look much like one!

Back to real Skylarks. It's not always appreciated that this is a highly migratory species and small, and sometimes large, flocks can be seen travelling during the day, overland and along the coasts and even way out over the sea. At such times their flap and glide style and slightly rounded wing tips always remind me of Redwings . . . but maybe that's just the way I see it. When distinguishing between different larks and the different pipits, including the rare ones, get to know the appropriate habitats (as always) and listen hard, especially to the pipits. Calls can clinch it! (Good birder's motto that.)

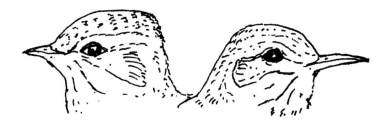

One of these birds has no crest, the other definitely *has . . .*
. . . so which is which?

Young Yellow Wag and Tawny Pipit. But which is which?

SWIFTS, SWALLOWS AND MARTINS

No real problems with outside confusion species – I don't *think* so anyway. (As long as you don't mistake displaying Ringed Plovers for Alpine Swifts) and the same goes for the

WAGTAILS

(though young Yellow Wags look rather like the rare **Tawny Pipit**) and

WAXWING

Although I can't resist a note on this one. It's another of those species birders seek out and non-birders see (like Hoopoes)! A very expert ornithologist told me how a neighbour of his called him to say she'd got this 'funny bird' in her garden. He asked her to describe it and she did. The colours came thick, fast and confusing: 'It was brown but it had yellow in the wings' . . . 'A Goldfinch?' . . . 'Black on the face.' . . . 'A Siskin perhaps?' . . . 'Red on it somewhere.' . . . 'Back to Goldfinch.' . . . 'Black and white wings' . . . 'Great Spotted Woodpecker?' . . . 'Bit of a crest.' . . . 'Ah, a Jay'. . . . One by one she looked them all up in her book. 'No . . . no . . . no. . . .' My friend was stumped. 'I don't know *what* it is,' he confessed. 'Neither do I,' she agreed. 'But whatever it is, it's finished off all my Cotoneaster berries.' 'Try Waxwing,' he suggested. 'That's *it!*' 'Hang on, I'll be right over.' 'Oh, it's gone now.'

I don't know a better story to illustrate the point that feeding habits can often be *the* vital piece of information. On the other hand, please don't assume any bird eating Cotoneaster berries *must* be a Waxwing!

WREN

Rarely have such little birds caused such big problems! Wrens occur everywhere. You certainly get them in gardens and local parks; you also get them out in the bracken on windy headlands or flitting along rocks and drystone walls on remote islands. Wherever small brown rare **warblers** occasionally turn up, Wrens are always present, and they are much more numerous. What's more, Wrens make little chacking and ticking noises very similar to the sounds these rare warblers are supposed to make and presumably do, if we're ever lucky enough to hear them. So . . . a sombre warning to rarity hunters. I'm sure *you'd* never do it but I am absolutely certain that many a wild warbler chase has been sparked off by a dodgy sighting of a Wren. It's the head-end to watch out for.

Nearly everything but . . .

Wrens have little warbler-like bills, and whitish eyestripes – just like many warblers. Add to this skulking habits and 'little brown job' plumage that can vary from olive to chestnut depending on the light and it all adds up to a naughty little species.

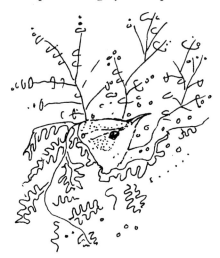

The 'naughty end'
of a Wren . . .
but definitely NOT
a rare warbler.

Look at the rare warbler pages in the field guide and like as not the text won't mention Wren but believe me . . . Cetti's Warbler, Dusky, Radde's, Paddyfield, Lanceolated and so on – they've all got a little bit of Wren in them – just make sure you recognize it!

DUNNOCK

And appropriately enough the Dunnock may well be the next naughtiest. Repeat the Wren warning: Dunnocks occur everywhere, they skulk and at a fleeting glimpse they can look a bit like all sorts of **elusive warblers**, particularly the streakier ones like Grasshopper and Lanceolated. And to finish off a truly notorious trio. . . .

ROBIN

The Robin! 'How can this be?' you ask. The most popular and most easily recognized bird in the land. From the front, yes – that red breast yells out instant Christmas card (though it *has* been mistaken for a Red-breasted Flycatcher on more than one occasion) but from the back. . . .

Aha, now this is a different matter. The Robin is in fact one of *the* most versatile confusion species. Like Wrens and Dunnocks, they can occur in all habitats, especially on migration, and they are equally brown and nondescript, if not more so. But most impressive of all, they have a greater range of impersonations in the way they fly. Seen for more than a second or two, Wrens do tend to give themselves away by their whirring wings, and Dunnocks too have a distinctive 'pumping' style. Robins, however, seem to be able to flit blithely like **warblers**, or dive like **small thrushes**, or **Nightingales**, *and* they can cascade like flycatchers, and even dash along the ground like **Bluethroats**. They also have a fair old repertoire of not always immediately recognizable 'ticks' and 'tacks'. All in all, I reckon that I've had more 'what was *that?*' moments from Robins than any other species. Fortunately, they do also have a habit of re-appearing and perching close by, and turning round to look at you, and flashing the red breast. So let's be grateful for that. However, don't forget very young Robins *don't have* a red breast – it's all speckly. But it's not long before Christmas card plumage starts showing through.

Only a Robin.

NIGHTINGALE

I feel a bit guilty writing this one but I feel I have to: ornithological accuracy has to overcome sentiment. There's an elderly lady who lives opposite me in North London. Last February she popped a little note through my door. *'Dear Mr Oddie, I thought you'd like to know there was a Nightingale singing in my garden yesterday.'* I didn't reply. Next day I got another note. *'Nightingale singing again last night.'* For two days, no further news. Then another message. *'Early this morning the Nightingale was singing on the roof of Number 24.'* Still I hadn't the heart to reply. Then I got the one I couldn't ignore. I was sitting in my office. I heard the front door letterbox clang. I tiptoed downstairs. I unfolded the note: *'The Nightingale is singing on the roof of Number 24 – now.'*

I scuttled back upstairs and peered out of the window. I looked across the road to where my neighbour lives. The lace curtains trembled and her bright-eyed little face appeared. She looked across and beamed at me as her trembling finger pointed to the roof of Number 24. On which, silhouetted against the February dusk, singing away happily . . . was a Blackbird. I looked back at her. Smiled and nodded. I never wrote about it to her or anyone else. Not until now. The truth is, my neighbour is by no means the only one to let me know they're being serenaded by Nightingales. However the fact is: Nightingales are summer visitors. They don't arrive until well into April, chances are they don't sing much at all after let's say, mid June, and they're off back to Africa in August and September. So, they do not occur in Britain in wintry months at all. Furthermore, they really are very local and are, sadly, restricted to only a few woodland areas south of a line from Lincolnshire to Devon. So, be honest, the chances of one singing in the middle of any city in February are nil. False Nightingales are, however, one of *the* commonest reports – they even get into *The Times* along with the first Cuckoos – and one of the reasons is that there is a popular misconception that anything singing at night *must* be a Nightingale. Well, by no means. *Several* species sing at night both in the town and in the country – so imposters can occur in woodlands too. The commonest night singers are Blackbird, Song Thrush and that old dissembler, the Robin. Of these the Blackbird and Song Thrush have particularly rich songs and indeed could be said to rival the Nightingales – and that's no disrespect to Robins who aren't bad either. So it's really not unreasonable for a non-birder to hear any of these three warbling away well after midnight and assume they've got Nightingales – but chances are they haven't. The Nightingale that sang in Berkeley

Square was probably a Blackbird . . . just flown over from the roof of Number 24.

Of course I'm writing all this not because I imagine anyone reading this book would or could make such a mistake . . . it's just that next time somebody tells you they've heard a Nightingale you can put them right. But I warn you, they'll be *ever* so disappointed.

REDSTART AND BLACK REDSTART

Once you've seen the tail they're no real trouble, though it's always a bit of a shock to glimpse that flash of scarlet. Mind you, in the middle of a built up area it's also a great delight, and odds on it's a **Black Redstart** there, not its country cousin. Again though, remember both *can* occur in the same sort of areas on migration. Without the tail, as it were, and perched on a fence, for example, female and young Redstarts have an upright pose that can resemble a **Wheatear** or **Whinchat** or even a **Spotted Flycatcher**. It's only a momentary illusion though, they're rarely still for long and once they fly – there's that flickering tail giving them away.

WHINCHAT, STONECHAT AND WHEATEAR

I'm dealing with these together as they all belong to the thrush family and share some similarities in jizz especially when they perch on top of fences, gorse or bracken which they all do. Wheatears, more often seen on the ground, can be easily 'thrown away' as Whinchats at a distance. Again though one short flight, flashing their white rumps, gives them away.

I have known Whinchats and Stonechats misidentified for an odd range of rarities though I suspect it doesn't happen often. A suspected **Red-breasted Flycatcher** in Northumberland turned out to be a Whinchat . . .

A bird against the skyline is a silhouette; against a rock it becomes a Wheatear. Sometimes moving only a few yards will make all the difference.

orange on the throat, white in the tail, maybe even flycatching a bit? And I once heard of a **Red-flanked Bluetail** from Blakeney Point in Norfolk that was never traced to anything more possible than a Stonechat. Come to think of it, a *female* Bluetail . . . yes, really quite like a female Stonechat . . . except for the blue tail of course . . . and except for the fact that it's only ever occurred in Britain half-a-dozen times (the Bluetail that is).

Wheatears are indeed extremely distinctive. Nothing else has that white rump, and even front-on as they run across open ground – scurrying, stopping, looking up and around – they stand out a mile. However, it is perhaps worth noting that several field guides mention their habitat as 'moorlands, downs, brecks and so on', omitting the fact that on migration Wheatears often appear on rather less glamorous inland substitutes, especially playing fields and golf courses. Actually though, my favourite Wheatear sighting was glamorous indeed . . . hopping along the pitch at Lords cricket ground just after close of play of the commemorative Test between the MCC and the Rest of the World!

Female or young birds perched or peeping out over a wall can have a momentary look of **Whinchats**, female **Redstarts**, or even **Spotted Fly-catchers**, but it doesn't last long.

Three typical fence perchers – Whinchat, Stonechat and Spotted Flycatcher.

Males are pretty unmistakable but I have been on a hunt for a **Lesser Grey Shrike** in Shetland when a male Wheatear popping its head over a rock solicited a yell of 'There it is' . . . and yes, they are both grey on top, with black masks . . . but then again everyone was getting a bit over-excited!

'BIG THRUSHES': Song and Mistle Thrush, Ring Ouzel, Redwing and Blackbird

Apart from the rather extraordinary case of the Mistle Thrush and the Nightjar (see Nightjar, page 138) most confusions are likely to be *within* the group, as it were, so I feel justified in referring you to the field guides. I can't resist a few memories though. **Juvenile** and **female Blackbirds** have been the cause of several misdirected twitches in their time. Juveniles can be very spotty, and therefore resemble some odd thrush – and females can be surprisingly rufous. Occasionally you get both, and then maybe a rumour of a '**possible American Robin**'. Also beware of partial **albino Blackbirds** with white blotches that can certainly make them vaguely resemble **Ring Ouzels**. It's really just a matter of accurate observation and

Both just 'funny' Blackbirds.

being honest: that patch of white, is it *really* symmetrically across the breast? Is that bird really rich chestnut colour? Couldn't it *really* just be a 'funny blackbird'?

WARBLERS

I suppose when people talk of 'little brown jobs' they probably mean warblers. No one can pretend it's not a difficult group but as with waders or raptors you can encourage youoself by having a quick flip through the field guide and crossing off those you *do* definitely know. Under 'battle conditions' in the field the process of elimination method is to be recommended, and certainly constantly bear in mind what you're likely to see in particular habitats. Having said that, I'm afraid warblers more than any other group do pop up in the 'wrong' places on migration. Chiffchaffs and Willow Warblers simply love flitting around in reed beds in the autumn, and I once watched a Reed Warbler in a gorse bush halfway down a cliff on Lundy Island in spring where I had every right to assume it would turn out to be something much rarer! At least there's not much outside the warbler family that can cause problems once you've had a decent view. However if you *haven't* had a decent view – please first make sure you've dismissed **Robin**, **Dunnock** and **Wren** from the possibles list. After that, and you're sure it *is* a warbler, then it's down to the process of elimination and narrowing it down to groups. It's one time

I really would recommend the technical terms – or rather the group Latin names. For years I was intimidated by heavy birdwatchers talking about 'phylloscs', 'acros' and even 'hippos'. Surely no-one could mistake a hippo!? That *would* cause a twitch on Blakeney Point. Eventually I plucked up courage to ask for a translation.

It wasn't as confusing as I'd thought. It turned out that what I'd been calling Willow/Chiffs – because I couldn't be sure if they were Chiffchaffs or Willow Warblers – came under the scientific heading of *Phylloscopus* warblers. Generally they were the little olive green and yellowy ones that preferred woodlands. So it came as no great surprise that Wood Warbler was a *Phylloscopus* too. Reed and Sedge Warblers had their group too – *Acrocephalus* – and Whitethroat, Lesser Whitethroat were *Sylvias* and so on. It helped, because it was all a sort of shorthand and indeed a short-cut when faced with a problem of warbler identification in the field. First step – assign it to its group, and the possibilities are narrowed down very considerably. Since you're bound to be under pressure most of the long scientific names have been abbreviated to 'Phyllosc', 'Acro' and indeed 'Hippo', which is short for the *Hippolais* group. Now, I'm certainly not going to attempt to elucidate the subtleties of warbler identification here. The field guides generally do it pretty well, and there have been some excellent articles in specialist magazines like *British Birds* and *Bird Watching*. As yet though I don't think there *is* a truly excellent book on warbler identification alone to rival *Waders*, *Seabirds* and *Birds of Prey*. No doubt there *will* be before long, and not before time. Also, I have to say that the jizz of warblers is notoriously hard to capture in an illustration, perhaps because so much of it is to do with the way the birds move. This, coupled with the fact that important plumage details are often very subtle, means that even some of the best field guides are weakest in the warbler department.

Nevertheless it's all good fun, if only for the arguments that can develop between birdwatchers when a tricky warbler is sighted. There have been some notorious birds that have defied identification until actually trapped and measured. So, the first lesson has to be: please don't panic if you can't immediately put a name to a warbler you see. Assume it's a common one until proved otherwise; listen out for any noises – snatches of song are usually diagnostic but not all calls are; think about what it 'ought to be' and first and foremost try and assign it to its correct group. Talking of which, here is a simplified list of those groups and their abbreviations. It's all implied in the field guides but it isn't usually laid out quite like this so I hope it may be of some use.

Phylloscopus warblers: 'Phylloscs'
Willow Warbler, Chiffchaff, Wood Warbler (plus rarities such as Yellow-browed, Greenish, Arctic, Pallas's). Fast dainty flyers, often given to flycatching, generally favour woodlands and large trees.

Sylvia warblers
Small Sylvias: Whitethroat, Lesser Whitethroat (and related rarities such as Dartford, Subalpine, Sardinian etc). Prefer low scrubby vegetation, gorse and brambles. Fast movers, often slightly scruffy look, may 'cock' tails. Larger Sylvias: Garden Warbler and Blackcap (rarities include Barred Warbler). Slow movers, which feed and sing in middle sized or even tall trees but breed in lower bushes and are seen in scrub on migration.

Acrocephalus warblers: 'Acros'
Unstreaked Acros: Reed and Marsh Warblers (rarities include Great Reed, Blyth's Reed, Paddyfield).

Streaked Acros: Sedge Warbler (rarities, Aquatic and Moustached Warblers).

All basically water warblers, preferring damp areas reeds, brambles near water, ditches etc. . . .

Locustellas (no, not 'Locusts'!)

Streaked: Grasshopper Warbler (rarities include Lanceolated and Pallas's Grasshopper)

Unstreaked: the uncommon Savi's Warbler (and the very rare River Warbler).

'Watery' warblers again, preferring reed beds, or short damp vegetation. Very skulking. They hop or even run along the ground; although they are all capable of shinning up reeds or perching in bushes to sing.

Hippolais 'Hippos'
All migrants in Britain and all scarce. The commonest (though still rare) are Icterine and Melodious Warblers. The *real* rarities include Olivaceous and Booted. Slow movers, usually in bushes or lower branches of trees. In jizz not dissimilar to 'Acros', especially Reed Warbler types.

And finally . . . Cetti's Warbler, in a group of its own.

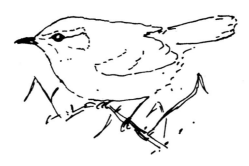

So really that's not *too* daunting. Well, I hope not.

May I suggest you browse through the illustrations in the field guide and assign the birds to their groups, as it were, look at the pictures, read the notes, and become conscious of what the related species have in common. Then next time you're out looking at warblers do the same with the real things. . . . If you find yourself muttering to yourself 'acro . . . phyllosc . . . sylvia . . . ' that's fine – in fact it'll probably impress other birdwatchers no end!

FLYCATCHERS

It's always a bit of a relief when birds' names remind you what to look for! Flycatchers do indeed catch flies and they do so in a suitably acrobatic style. Beware though that several other species do the same (though not quite so deftly perhaps). 'Phylloscs' (remember them?) are particularly agile, and I've even seen **sparrows, Starlings** and **Black-headed Gulls** having a go (though if you mistake *them* for a flycatcher you know a lot less than I think you do!). What really does distinguish a flycatcher is the way it repeatedly returns to the same perch, where it sits in a characteristically upright pose until it flits off after the next fly. It's perhaps a good thing they *are* so distinctive, as I often think that if **Spotted Flycatchers** hopped along the ground they'd be mistaken for all sorts of things – after all they're another one that's brown and streaky.

As it is I can think of only a few confusions. A Spotted Fly, being fairly chunky and greyish brown, if seen flitting around a bush can be fleetingly reminiscent of a **Garden Warbler** or **Blackcap**, or if it's on rocks, a **Rock Pipit**.

Some days everything's a flycatcher. Here it's young Pied Wagtails and a few distant Black-headed Gulls.

And, as I've already warned, **Robins, Whinchats** and **Stonechats** have been misreported as the rare **Red-breasted Flycatcher**, which believe me is another one in the 'when you see it you'll know' category (even though it's very unlikely to have a red breast – only full breeding adults have that).

GOLDCREST AND FIRECREST

Only really confusable with small *Phylloscopus* warblers, especially the youngest juveniles who haven't yet developed their crests.

TITS

A wondrously unmistakable group and even pretty easy to tell from one another except the notorious Marsh and Willow Tit pair. I won't go into that, as all the field guides do. All I would say is learn those calls as most tits are hard to see flitting up in the trees. There are lots of little soft 'seeps' that are hard to distinguish but most species also make some easily recognized noises. **Great Tits** though are bewilderingly inventive and always seem to be coming up with something you've never heard before. It's a not altogether frivolous rule to say: 'If you don't recognize it – it's a Great Tit'!

NUTHATCH AND TREECREEPER

Another couple of easy ones

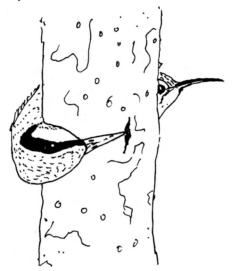

and . . .

GOLDEN ORIOLE

Which *should* be easy . . . and indeed if you see a male I don't think you'll mistake it. As I've already warned though **Green Woodpeckers** flying away and showing yellow rumps are often misidentified as female Orioles. Many of the field guides say that Golden Orioles much prefer being up hidden in the trees and in breeding areas this is indeed true. However, my experience of Orioles on migration is that they very often choose to feed on the ground or low down. For example on the island of Tresco in the Scillies there are plenty of huge trees and yet whenever I've seen Orioles there they've been down in the gorse or flitting ahead of me on the hillside paths, looking very much like a Green Woodpecker flushed from an ant hill. Fortunately, there's no Green Woodpeckers on Scilly to confuse the issue!

I suppose I should give one final Oriole warning – their fluty song is extremely distinctive but it is possible to impersonate it by slowly pulling out the handle of a bicycle pump . . . so if you think you hear a Golden Oriole just make sure it isn't a *schoolboy with a flat tyre*!

SHRIKES: Red-backed, Great Grey, Lesser Grey and Woodchat

Sadly, all shrikes are now pretty rare birds. There still may be a few pairs of Red-backs breeding in Britain but if you get to hear about them, *please* leave them alone. So if you are lucky enough to see a shrike it'll probably be on migration, in spring or autumn or maybe a wintering **Great Grey**. The one I think could most easily be overlooked is female or juvenile **Red-backed**. They really are surprisingly dull, and perhaps not as big as one expects.

Furthermore, there is a bit of a fallacy amongst birdwatchers that shrikes are almost invariably seen perching on telegraph wires and fence posts. The truth is, I think, that that is where they're most often seen because that's where they're most conspicuous. In fact Red-Backs in particular spend much of their time on brambles, small bushes, or hedgerows where they are much less obvious. If they're hunched up and static, brown Red-backs or indeed juvenile **Woodchats** could as easily pass for sleepy female **House Sparrows** or even lumps of mud! So, that's my advice if you ever go on a shrike-twitch: don't just look at the obvious perches, scan along the low vegetation, and rocks and walls as well, and don't give up easily. Shrikes are great disappearers, so if you arrive only to be told 'it's gone' – come back later and try again. It is often assumed that shrikes are faithful to favourite perches. Well, if you're lucky it may be true but I had a frustrating example of just how elusive they can be several years ago on Out Skerries.

It was late May and there was quite a fall of migrants including several Red-backed Shrikes and among them a single rarity – which eventually turned out to be a Lesser Grey. At first glimpse though it was only a 'grey shrike', disappearing over the brow of a hill . . . it was several hours before we saw it again, during which time the heads of several Red-backs and a couple of male Wheatears gave us various false alarms. The bird was then sighted some 150 yards away, perched on top of a small pile of

Both grey-headed; both masked.

stones at the bottom of a valley: a perfect 'favourite perch' if ever I saw one. The heat haze was distorting our view so much we *still* weren't absolutely sure if we had a Great or a Lesser Grey. So we galloped behind the cover of the hillside to emerge just above the pile of stones. We peeped over. No shrike. It was another day or two before we saw it again. This time perched on a signpost and close enough to be sure of our identification. But still it didn't settle. Over a period of about a week it was seen maybe half a dozen times – and never in the same place twice. Any twitcher dropping in for an afternoon would almost certainly have missed it.

It's not a bad lesson for rarities in general but I think it's particularly applicable to shrikes – they *do* fly and they don't always stick to their favourite spot. Fortunately though – *some* do!

And they don't always perch on fence posts.

JAY

The Jay deserves a prize as the bird most often reported by non-birders. If anyone ever writes to me, calls me, or stops me in the street and says 'I've got this funny bird in my garden', my immediate response is to assume it's a Jay (unless of course it's singing from the top of the roof of Number 24). What is interesting is how varied the descriptions can be: 'It's pink' . . . 'It's black and white' . . . 'It's bright blue'. . . 'It's got a white rump' . . . 'It's got a crest' . . . and so on. All of which is true. The layman's description, however, rarely contains *all* of that, and it's surprising how difficult it would be to identify the bird from the information given. Feed these snippets to the computer and it'd come up with everything from a Hoopoe to a Brambling. It all goes to show just how thorough a description needs to be for it to be totally recognizable or indeed acceptable to a rarities committee.

Fortunately the bird itself *is* pretty recognizable so if you ever find yourself approached by the person who's seen the 'funny bird' show them a plateful of Jays from a good field guide and with any luck they'll say 'that's it.'

MAGPIE

If you can't recognize a Magpie . . . take up train spotting.

OK. So which is the Magpie and which is the train?

THE BLACK CROWS: Chough and Jackdaw

Choughs are another 'when you see it you'll know' species – and indeed when you hear it. They are very local, being restricted to coastal bits of Wales and Ireland so it's likely that's where you'll be when you're looking for them. Chances are you'll also be looking hard at a thousand Jackdaws too, wondering if you'll be able to pick out your Chough among them. Take heart, you *will*. Theoretically they ought to be quite hard to separate as they're tossed about in a windy sky, but there is something about those raggedy wings that is instant Chough and their exploding-cough of a call is not a bit like a Jackdaw.

Rooks, Crows and Raven

There's an old country cliché – 'if you see a bunch of crows in a field – they're Rooks.' Not entirely true, but not a bad general rule. Crows *are* less gregarious but you do get small flocks sometimes. Beware though of thinking you've found a field-full of crows in autumn – young **Rooks** have black beaks too, so concentrate on head shape and the Rooks' 'shaggy trousers'.

If you're looking for **Ravens** make sure you're in the right place (and I don't mean the Tower of London) – crags and cliffs to the west side of Britain. It's a bit like the Buzzard and eagle problem. Think of Ravens as the eagles of the crow family – they're much rarer and much bigger than crows. Look out for that diamond-shaped tail and listen for that wonderful gruff croak.

The problems always arise with single birds soaring high on the wind, or circling in the thermals, or tumbling over distant horizons – suddenly size is hard to judge. Crows can look like Ravens and vice versa and both can look like **distant raptors** . . . and indeed vice versa.

As I said when discussing birds of prey, if you're with other bird-watchers don't be shy about pointing out *anything* big on the horizon. Experts not only get their raptors mixed up sometimes, they certainly need to give the odd crow a second look too. (See page 67 again.)

STARLING

A best known if not always best loved bird. No problem recognizing adults, though the **brown juveniles** sometimes puzzle beginners. Remember it's not only in city centres you'll see flocks of Starlings. Rather like

*Unmistakable silhouettes . . .
except for the two sparrows.*

Skylarks, a large percentage of the population is highly migratory and in autumn and early winter they come streaming in over our coastlines. At such times small parties can be confused with **Redwings** but the Starling flaps more frantically on noticeably sharper-tipped wings.

SEED-EATERS: Finches, Buntings, Sparrows

HOUSE AND TREE SPARROW

Tree Sparrows are only really confusable with male **House Sparrows** so have a look at the book. **Female House Sparrows** though are quite versatile little mimics. They don't mean to be I'm sure, but it just happens that there are several other species that can, at a casual glimpse, be passed over as female House Sparrows. They *are* pretty nondescript – basically browny grey with various bits of streaking and just bulky enough to look quite big when they're fluffed up or quite small if they're well preened. I've already mentioned the possibility of overlooking a dull and **distant shrike.**

Moreover, sparrows are capable of lumbering around in deep cover and conjuring thoughts of large **warblers,** and on sunny days I've even caught them **flycatching.** More likely though most sparrow confusion species are other seed-eaters, notably dull female **Greenfinches,** and particularly the rare **Scarlet Rosefinch** which is invariably anything but scarlet, in fact it's distinctly sparrow-coloured. Being numerous and adaptable, sparrows do get just about everywhere and, especially in autumn when even the males look pretty mousy, there have certainly been days when I wished they didn't exist at all. When you're searching for a single rare 'little brown job' you can't help thinking the quest would be a lot easier if there weren't quite so many sparrows in the world, or worse still in the fields you're looking through.

Having said that, a couple of words in praise of sparrows. Many a rarity has been found in a flock of House Sparrows and their very sociability sometimes persuades the vagrant to stay longer than it might otherwise. Rare-bird reports often refer to 'the bird habitually fed with sparrows'. It thereby follows that it's worth sorting through such flocks in case there's a foreigner amongst them. And if you do find 'something good' be grateful that the sparrow provides us with such an instantly acceptable size comparison. I sometimes think how much less graphic

Preening time for House Sparrows.

descriptions would be if we couldn't write 'sparrow-sized' or 'slightly smaller/ bigger than a sparrow'. Even the computer understands that one.

FINCHES

The rest of the finch family contains some of our most distinctive males and some of the least distinguished or distinguishable female and juveniles. Fortunately, those little seed-eating beaks, and the feeding habits of the birds will almost always very soon lead you to the right pages in the books and then it's a matter of becoming aware of the possible confusions which often come in pairs – female **Chaffinches** and **Bramblings** . . . **Twite** and **Linnet** . . . **Redpoll** and **Siskin** and so on.

A word about **Crossbills**. It's a local species and generally recorded in known conifer plantations and woodlands. It's likely therefore that you'll visit one of these places hoping and expecting to see birds you know are there somewhere. Well, that's what I did anyway. Beware of **Greenfinches**! Not only do female and young Crossbills look rather like dull Greenfinches (and female **House Sparrows**!), the Crossbill call, which you've probably been told to listen out for, is hard to describe in any way that doesn't make it sound almost identical to one of the

Greenfinch's flight calls. Most books put them both down as 'jip' or 'chip' or 'djup' . . . whilst adding that the Crossbill is 'more explosive'. (Personally, I've never actually seen a Crossbill explode!) The fact is, eventually you'll see a small party of birds in the tops of the trees nibbling away on the pine cones and they will indeed be Crossbills . . . and then they'll call and you'll say 'yes that's like a Greenfinch . . . but different' . . . and hopefully from then on it'll stick in your mind. Just be prepared for a few irritating Greenfinches first. And before you start having visions of rare **Two-barred Crossbills**, remember there are probably lots of **Chaffinches** in the same wood, all of which have 'two bars'.

Talking of which, I have to admit as a youngster (and I *was* pretty young) I optimistically once kidded myself that a very distant Chaffinch

was a **Hawfinch**. Apart from anything else it was perched up on top of a big tree in a hedgerow. This alone proves it couldn't possibly have been a Hawfinch, as Hawfinches are almost never *seen* at all, let alone out in the open. In the whole of my thirty-odd years' birdwatching I have only ever *seen* about a dozen Hawfinches and only one of them well . . . and come to think of it that wasn't *really* well. It was in the middle of a thick wood fifteen feet directly above my head – and as it flew off I fell over backwards into a patch of nettles. I have *heard* a few more. They make a ticking noise that you could easily not notice because it sounds very like a **Robin**. The books call them 'very shy'. I should say so. For years I wondered if they existed at all!

One last 'silly one' on finch misidentification. I once followed up a report of an '**American warbler**' on Scilly only to discover a **Siskin** in the same bush. Actually it's not that silly – you have a look at a page of American warblers, all stripey with bits of yellow, very like Siskins come to think of it . . . and come to think of it again, knowing the Scillies, it's perfectly possible there *was* an American warbler in there as well . . . oh dear, what did I miss? Oh well, I'll have another look next time I'm on St Mary's.

So . . . which is which?

BUNTINGS

Rather like the finches, the males are generally no trouble: but the females and juveniles – well, we mentioned them earlier as amongst the quintessential 'little brown jobs'.

We also mentioned the possible momentary similarities to larks and pipits (see larks and pipits) but fortunately otherwise as a family buntings are not hard to recognize. They have finch-like, seed-eating beaks, but are generally sleeker than the finches, particularly in that they have longer tails which in most cases (but not quite all) are edged in white.

It's fair to say that all the difficult female buntings are basically brownish and streaked both above and below. The differences are indeed subtle and usually consist of small areas of colour usually on the face, flanks, wings, breast or rump – so those are the areas to concentrate on when faced with a nondescript Bunting you can't put a name to. The thing to bear in mind is that these colours are *not* bright: we're talking about different shades of brown, or gentle washes of yellow or russet, so look hard. You also need to be accurate about *where* the colours or markings are: 'somewhere on the wing' is rarely specific enough. It's now that those feather names really come into use (see page 42).

Stare at a whole page full of rare Buntings and it can be pretty intimidating, but stick to the 'common ones' and it's really not so frightening at all.

Let's assume we're at the southeast coast, on stubbly ground in late autumn – now at that time and in that place more or less any of the less rare Buntings might well occur. We'll even assume that they are going to be in dull juvenile or female-looking plumage.

Snow Buntings are pretty easy, whatever the sex. So that's one down. Now let's work on the 'assume it's common' principle. Surprisingly, and I hope encouragingly, you're down to only three species already, and they're not difficult to tell from one another.

The species are Reed Bunting, Yellowhammer and Corn Bunting. Let's 'get rid of' Corn Bunting – it's rather bulky and hasn't really got any obvious markings at all and most significantly it doesn't have any white in its tail. We're perhaps used to seeing and hearing Corn Buntings jangling and rattling from their song perches, but they *do* occur hopping around on the ground too. Not a bad rule, if your mystery bird seems particularly featureless: have you considered Corn Bunting? Check that tail. OK. So now we're down to Reed Bunting and Yellowhammer. Consider them next, remembering especially that male Reed Buntings moult into winter plumage and sometimes show varying degrees of black markings round their heads. However, if you feel your bird is neither Reed Bunting or Yellowhammer (remember, we're considering only juveniles or females) . . . what next?

Well, rather conveniently, these two speices act as appropriate basic types for the rarer ones.

If the bird is rather coarsely marked with blackish streaks on the back and wings then it belongs to the 'Reed Bunting' group as it were. Of the reasonably common species left to consider there's only Lapland Bunting, and that's pretty scarce. ('Laps' usually give themselves away by their scurrying lark-like movements.)

If the bird is less coarse and has gentler brownish streaks you can assign it to the 'Yellowhammer' type . . . in which case the only *relatively* common species are Ortolan Bunting (a scarce migrant) or Cirl Bunting (a very localized breeding bird). If you still can't find your problem bunting you then have to go on to the real rarities. In many cases you'll find the two groupings still apply. Coarser birds include Little and Rustic Buntings, subtler ones would include Yellow-breasted and Pine Buntings.

A 'Lap' – a mass of head stripes: supercilium, subcoronal, eyestripe, ear coverts, moustachial etc.

Remember though that by now you really are dealing with very rare birds. In many places and at most times there really are only two or three likely species.

I'm not going to go into all the identification features of all the buntings now – again it's all in those excellent field guides – but I do hope what I've just written will just help you a bit going through the identification process and narrowing them down.

AFTERTHOUGHT

I've just read through this last section. I quite enjoyed it actually! I hope you did. One thing bothered me a bit though: I do hope I haven't put you off by making things seem more difficult than they are. Let me re-assure you on two points. Firstly, the *majority* of the birds you'll see are not hard to identify, and secondly, the process of working out the more difficult ones is actually very satisfying. It's a challenge and meeting it really is great fun. The 'notes and tips' I've given nearly all apply to birds you don't see very well – at a distance, flying away, deep in cover and so on. Believe me, there is nothing more gratifying than being able to put a name to a bird on even the briefest of glimpses. It's a great moment when it hops out and reveals itself to be exactly what you thought it was. Usually of course it'll be something reasonably common. Now and then though – it'll be something really rare.

Which brings me to a question that concerns most modern bird-watchers. . . .

. . . something really rare?

To Twitch
or not to Twitch?

Nowadays there can't be many people who are not familiar with the word 'Twitcher' – which only goes to show how popular this form of birdwatching has become in recent years. However, in case you've managed to avoid the subject I'll just define the process. A twitcher is mainly concerned with seeing rare birds. Most, if not all, of his or her birdwatching consists of finding out what's around and then travelling to see it, sometimes considerable distances. Wealthy (or unemployed?) twitchers think nothing of spending October whisking themselves between Scilly and Shetland and all points in between. Less obsessive travellers will still spend every weekend racing around the country chasing the rarities rather than working a local patch. Twitchers tend to keep a lot of lists. The main priority is a British Life List which is usually extended to include southern Ireland – which is a good idea since quite a few rare birds turn up there. In addition they'll probably keep a World List, and a European or Western Palearctic List.

The driving incentive to twitch is the possibility of adding a new 'tick' to any of these lists. You can also create less significant incentives by keeping more restricted lists: a year list, a month list, and, of course, in the case of a 24 hour bird-race, a day list. I must confess I have, to enliven an otherwise uneventful afternoon, even kept an hour list! You can also keep trip lists on bird holidays, and train-journey lists make a pleasant alternative to listening to your Walkman – although actually you can do both at the same time. I think my most productive trip was from Plymouth to London. Nearly 60 species and five-and-a-half cassettes worth of music! Come to think of it, train-twitching is one of the few ways I can think of that you can actually learn to look forward to being held up by points-failures – it's about the only chance you get to tick off tits and warblers. I also keep a garden list and a Hampstead Heath list. Nevertheless, I'd like to take this opportunity, once and for all, to state that *I am not a twitcher*.

I have *written* about twitching at some length, so if you want to know more of the language and lore I'll immodestly direct you towards . . . *Bill Oddie's Little Black Bird Book* (now appropriately available very cheaply in paperback). But I repeat, I myself have twitched no more than ten times in my life, unless I 'just happened' to be in the area for some other reason. For example, I just happened to be appearing in a TV show in Southampton at the same time as a Greater Sand Plover was appearing at Pagham Harbour so I went to see it. (It never came to see me though.) I have also been lucky enough to find a few birds that have started twitches; but otherwise, honestly and truly, I do not go twitching.

This is *not* because I disapprove of twitching. However, some people do.

There are usually two kinds of arguments against. One is that there have been tales of thoughtless and clumsy twitchers damaging crops or fences, antagonizing local people and indeed other birdwatchers by chasing tired migrants. That is, then, a practical objection. The other criticism is more 'philosophical'. Twitching is considered a facile and 'impure' form of birdwatching – akin to ornithological trainspotting.

Supporters of twitching will usually counter this by saying that *all* birdwatchers twitch to a point, and that there's no difference between rushing to your local reservoir to see a Black-necked Grebe and flying to Fair Isle for a Red-flanked Bluetail. I can't *entirely* agree with that. I *would* maintain that *everyone* enjoys seeing rare birds, but I reckon there's a special satisfaction about seeing them on your own patch, and anyway a local twitch like that is only an occasional occurrence. It's not what you do *all* the time. So let's just accept, when you're considering the ethics of twitching, that we're talking about the real thing – full-time rarity hunting.

So . . . are the complaints valid? Well, let's take the practical objection first, as it is much the more important. It cannot be denied that there have been a few instances of damage, distress and bad behaviour. Birds have been harassed perhaps most commonly by photographers trying to get one step nearer or by over-impatient birdwatchers who want to tick this one off so they can get on to the next. Certainly trespassing also has and still does now and then occur. However, I'm absolutely convinced that these incidents are few and far between and are usually exaggerated by local people or the press. Heaven knows, I can well appreciate the bewilderment of a farmer or even a householder waking up to find his or her territory invaded by an army of five hundred or more frantic birdwatchers mainly dressed in paramilitary type uniform and brand-ishing a veritable arsenal of optical equipment.

I remember the warden of Kenfig reserve describing the scene one morning when Britain's first Little Whimbrel turned up and found itself trapped on a golf course between two converging phalanxes of telescope bearers that resembled a re-enactment of the Battle of Trafalgar.

I can't entirely blame the bird for shooting vertically upward and disappearing over the horizon never to return. What I *do* blame it for is doing it less than an hour before I happened to drop in on my way to Cardiff for another co-incidental TV programme. Nevertheless, I am perfectly sure that by and large twitching is harmless and that on the vast majority of occasions twitchers behave themselves pretty well towards people, property and, most importantly, birds.

The whole 'sport' (if that's what it is) is now extremely well organized and has a very clear and widely published code of behaviour on which the primary rule is: 'The safety and welfare of the bird comes first at all times.'

The second objection – that twitching is somehow not 'proper bird-watching' – is perhaps less important, and yet more interesting.

One thing cannot be denied: there are many twitchers who are among the country's most brilliant birdwatchers. Their theoretical knowledge and practical ability is superb. On the other hand, one could call some of these people almost 'professional twitchers': maybe their jobs are actually connected with birdwatching, or they can afford a lot of time off from work, or they don't mind 'roughing it' most of the time in a more or less obsessional pursuit of birds. In any event, the point is, they have a great deal of field-experience of both rare and common birds and therefore it's more or less inevitable they are pretty hot stuff at identification. It's likely that they are *also* knowledgeable ornithologists, and maybe all-round naturalists too. There simply aren't enough rare birds around to be able to spend every day of the year twitching without learning a great deal more besides!

However, it's not these top twitchers that worry me. What we are seeing now is, I think, a generation of birdwatchers who *began* as twitchers and spend all their birding time, weekends and holidays, twitching. They have no local patch and indeed in many cases little knowledge of or interest in common birds. Certainly they need to *see* common birds if only to tick them off, but they do not take the time to study them, and, as I hope I've stressed often enough in this book, the basic training towards learning how to recognize rarities is to first acquire a thorough knowledge of the commoner species.

The problem – or maybe it's the attraction? – is that on a twitch you don't *need* to be able to identify the bird for yourself. Chances are you'll be watching in a crowd who'll lead you to it, show you exactly where it is, and of course you even knew what it was before you arrived! So, no problems – except that it might have got embarrassed at being stared at and flown away. The thing is, to be a twitcher you don't *have* to be any good – map reading is a more valuable skill than bird identification. You can even *buy* yourself a big list. I know perfectly well there are a few wealthy 'listers' (that's an American word, and a small clue to where *some* of these people come from) who spend a great deal of money travelling in search of rare birds and paying people to show them to them so they can tick them off. They *need* to be shown because some of them wouldn't recognize a Puffin from a Peewit (and they are *not* confusion species!). Not that wealth is a guarantee of ignorance – there are some very expert American mega-listers too. But to come back to earth and to Britain I've also met young English twitchers who've ticked off Rustic and Little Buntings but still 'need' a Lapland. I just hope they'll recognize it when they see it. But then again, maybe they won't have to; maybe there'll be a hundred other people all looking at it with them . . . maybe *nobody'll* recognize it! All I know is, for my personal taste I enjoyed the Lapland Bunting I spotted myself in a field in southern Ireland much more than the one I shared with twenty other people in Dorset. But then maybe that's *my* problem. Maybe I suffer from claustrophobia. Maybe I'm selfish, wanting to keep these birds to myself and a few friends.

Whatever the arguments against twitching, there are also plenty in favour – ask any twitcher. And if twitching turns you on – that's fine. Certainly you'll find the whole thing very easy to get into now that there's an excellent telephone information service on the latest sightings, plus a magazine and so on (see Appendix, page 188). However, may I please just make one last little suggestion, especially if you are a beginner? Don't *just* twitch. Try and make time to visit a local patch every now and then; or why not take *one* twitching holiday a year and the rest of the time stick to less frantic birding? I have a lot of friends who do just that: every October they take a couple of weeks on the Scillies and chase everything in sight – and quite a lot that isn't. They see a lot of good birds and meet a lot of nice people.

Or – if you simply can't resist the lure of the list – when you *do* go to tick off the next rarity, set yourself a little test. Say to yourself 'would I have been able to identify this if there was no-one else here?' Take a description, do a drawing, and make sure the answer is 'yes'. Wherever you are, please do obey the 'code of conduct', don't disturb the bird unnecessarily, and do be considerate to fellow twitchers. They won't be very understanding if you clap your hands so you can get a look at the wing pattern and scare the bird off altogether! Oh, and once you've got your tick, why not stick around and explore and enjoy the area and see if you can find anything else? It's a proven fact that whatever weather conditions produced one rarity often bring in another so surely it's worth a look? Remember I mentioned that Yellow-billed Cuckoo I found at Portland (see page 26)? I *like* mentioning it because I was really proud of myself for finding it – even if it *was* all down to luck and a decent telescope – and I found it particularly gratifying to drive past the field each day for a week and see a crowd, sometimes of a hundred or more, looking at 'my cuckoo'. What amazed me though was that so few people stayed to explore the wonderful habitat on the rest of Portland Bill, apart perhaps for a quick visit to the Observatory garden and probably to the nearby reserve at Radipole Lake.

The result was that I and a few other semi-residents had most of the area to ourselves whilst nearly a thousand birdwatchers nipped in, ticked off the Cuckoo and nipped off again. On the Saturday morning a considerable crowd appeared, but the bird didn't. By ten o'clock the official statement was 'the cuckoo has gone' and five minutes later so had all the twitchers. Leaving the handful of Portland regulars to enjoy a splendid fall of small migrants including Lapland Buntings, Barred Warblers and an Aquatic Warbler – now surely some of the twitchers needed *that* one! By Sunday morning they were back . . . but the Aquatic Warbler wasn't. I was tempted to think 'serves 'em right!'

A Peewit and a Puffin

Birdwatching in the rest of Europe and Beyond

As it happens, Britain may well be the best country in Europe for birds and I'll confess it kept me perfectly content and occupied for many years. In fact it was only in the late seventies that I took my first proper bird-holiday abroad. Mind you, since then I've rather made up for it and I have to admit I've become pretty hooked on foreign parts and exotic species.

Nevertheless, much of my holiday birding is still 'incidental' in so far as I'm with my wife and family and it would quite understandably be frowned on if I disappeared from dawn till dusk every day. In case some of you are in the same position let's start with this kind of situation, and let's assume that you're on a family holiday in Europe in the Mediterranean region. First requisite is a field guide that goes beyond Britain. So that lets out the excellent *Shell Guide*, but brings in several others. With even more species to consider, it's particularly vital that you use the little distribution maps, and when you think you've identified a particularly exotic bird just check up that it's supposed to occur near the Costa Brava and not just in Arctic Norway! If you want to know exactly what the birds you might see *really* look like get *Birds of the Mediterranean and Alps* with wonderful illustrations by Lars Jonsson.

The secret of building up a good holiday list is, as in the UK, to visit several different types of habitat. You don't, however, necessarily need to seek out special reserves and sanctuaries, which in any case are rather few and far between compared with 'back home'. Also I'm assuming your time is limited and that you can't go off for long long drives in search of birds. So let's consider where you might look.

Around Hotels and Villas

If you stay in bed late you may see nothing, but get up early and you'll be surprised at the birds that may be flitting about the rooftops or feeding in the gardens. Don't assume even the sparrows are 'ordinary' – they may be handsome Italian or Spanish Sparrows, and a clump of weeds is as likely to attract Serins as Goldfinches. Look along the telegraph wires for Swallows, Hoopoes and shrikes, down in the shrubs for warblers and buntings; and especially keep an eye on those little watery areas – by the edge of swimming pools, a leaky garden hose, or the early morning lawn sprinkler – and I'll guarantee you'll see birds coming down to drink there. It's not a bad rule round the sunbaked Med to say: 'Where there's water there'll probably be birds'. Which brings me to . . .

The Seashore, Estuaries and Marshes

The beach itself may well be birdless – gulls are scarce in this region – but if there's a rocky shoreline look out for Blue Rock Thrushes and Crag Martins along the cliffs. Most of the natural marshes have been drained and reclaimed but man-made lagoons or salt-pans (look for 'salinas' on the map) attract water birds, as do estuaries when the low tide exposes mud and sand banks. It's a pleasant surprise to find that the majority of the 'Ringed Plovers' round the Med turn out to be Kentish!

Open Farmland, Olive Groves etc

Sadly, homogenized modern farming and the widespread use of pesticides has rendered a lot of apparently lush agricultural areas something of an ornithological desert. Ironically, comparatively sparse-looking and scrubby areas can often be much more productive. Again, get up early to see elusive but delightful little birds like Sardinian, Dartford and Spectacled Warblers (all 'Sylvias', remember them?). And look out for the handsome male Black-eared Wheatears and the notoriously tricky females.

Mountainous Regions

Especially in spring, a trip up to cooler mountain air guarantees a riot of alpine flowers and spectacular and colourful birds that you definitely won't see down by the coast. Keep bird-watching out of the car window (unless of course you're the driver!). Look along the roadside for high altitude specialities like Alpine Accentors, Wallcreepers and Rock Thrushes, and out across the ravines for birds of prey hanging on the wind or soaring in the thermals – that's where you may well see eagles or vultures.

When is the Best Time?

There are birds for all seasons and of course at different times of the year you'll see different species, but undoubtedly the most exciting periods are spring and autumn when migration is in full swing. In late March, April and May, and from August to October anything can turn up anywhere. Some days the air is full of birds: look out to sea and there'll be long dark whisps of wildfowl or terns; the skies above you may be swirling with raptors or storks and clouds of screaming swifts; and the trees and bushes alive with little birds which will send you scurrying to your field guide to sort them out. But if you have to take your holiday in June or July don't despair. Remember a lot of birds that are common in other parts of Europe would be exciting rarities in Britain. Only last year I had to stop over in Madrid for an afternoon in mid-June. During a two-hour stroll round the airport perimeter I saw several Hoopoes, Crested Larks, and Serins, whilst a Woodchat fed from a roadsign and Pallid Swifts circled overhead. That lot would've caused a bit of a twitch back at Portland! I've often heard birdwatchers – especially men – moaning that they can't

Mind you, they're not easy to identify when wet!

possibly combine their hobby with a family holiday, but I think as long as you're not too ambitious it should be possible. If you think about it, it's rather co-operative of the birds to be most visible early in the morning, before most people get up, and again in the late afternoon, when the rest of the family may well be having a little siesta. So take your chances and see what you can see in the time available. Actually I could argue that it'll benefit the whole family. After all, there's nothing grumpier than a frustrated birdwatcher, so if you can get a few hours in every now and then I'm pretty sure you'll be much better company and everyone will be grateful. With any luck, you'll then be able to negotiate being allowed to go off for a week or two on . . .

The Real Bird-Holiday

Now obviously this could be anywhere between here and Australia and I can't possibly give you a rundown on birds and birding of everywhere worth visiting – which is more or less anywhere!

I will, though, give a few tips based on my own experience of foreign birding over the past few years. Firstly, if you're thinking of going off on your own, think again. Surely these trips are much more enjoyable when you can share the experiences and compare notes? And there's also a safety factor involved, which I'll come to later.

Next, do plan your possible route and get as much information as possible before you leave about where to go to see particular species. Nowadays, this is pretty easy as sites and species lists for many countries are advertised in *Bird Watching* and *British Birds*, and several short guides have been published. Mind you, having said that, don't let a mass of information blunt your own enterprise. Don't forget a lot of 'site-lists' are really only an account of where a particular group of birdwatchers happened to go when they first visited a country and looked around for themselves. For example, when I first planned to go to Cyprus I was given several specific sites for two local specialities: Cyprus Pied Wheatear and Cyprus Warbler. They were wonderfully detailed – 'turn left by the church, half a mile further on the path narrows, then take a small track to a water pump and behind that is a rusty tractor which Pied Wheatear uses as a display post.' This is true. It's also true that you could hardly miss either species unless you locked yourself in your hotel room and in fact even then you'd probably see them by looking out of the window. I've seen Pied Wheatears perched on the TV aerials and Cyprus Warblers hopping around in the lupins.

Cyprus Warbler and Pied Wheatear (it's on the TV aerial . . . honest!)

I also remember a splendid trip to Thailand where for several days we followed information that would supposedly lead us to that much sought after beauty with the name to match, the Siberian Rubythroat. Eventually, we saw two together, including a dazzling male, but it wasn't at any of the known sites – it was when we stopped and wandered off into an anonymous woodland to answer the call of nature! It's funny to think that particular spot may now have become a Rubythroat site. Actually I doubt it, as we really had no idea where we were! So the rule is: plan your trip, yes, but do make time to try a few places people haven't been before you.

A few warnings, that will be more or less appropriate depending on which country you are visiting. You may have to get used to being stared at and even followed. Usually this is merely curiosity – birdwatchers are regarded as a bit of a novelty. On the other hand, it's sadly true that some locals have cottoned on to the fact that binoculars and telescopes are worth quite a bit of money and there have been a number of thefts and muggings. This is one reason why it's generally safer to be with a partner or a small group. It's obviously also unwise to leave expensive gear visible on the back seat of a parked car. Also be aware of whether or not you are trespassing. If you're on private farmland it's likely to be more impolite than risky – though do watch out for aggressive dogs. (Even as I write this I'm looking forward to the last in a course of rabies injections!) Wherever you are, it's worth learning the local way of saying 'I am watching birds'. This is quite likely to provoke a shrug of bewilderment or disinterest or possibly even disbelief, but in many cases it'll at least be enough for you to be allowed to carry on. If you're carrying a field guide, flash that, or maybe a page from your notebook, especially if it contains a recognizable drawing of a bird. Now and again you'll be pleasantly surprised, as I was in Tunisia when a young farm worker accompanied me for the rest of the afternoon and – despite my dodgy French – we conducted a quite passable conversation about the various waders and wildfowl on the local marsh. Mind you, at the end of it he asked me for a tip. The extended hand is a universal language.

Being caught trespassing on private farmland can be embarrassing, but trespassing in a military zone can be very dangerous. Unfortunately, the world over, many excellent bird-spots *are* also used as firing ranges and the like. I suppose the birds find being bombed occasionally less disturbing then being constantly chased by twitchers! I can't stress strongly enough though that if you go creeping round a 'sensitive' area – and this, alas, includes many civil airports – with binoculars and cameras you really are asking for trouble. At least you'll get warned off, at worst you could be shot at or arrested. I made this point earlier when I was discussing birdwatching clothing and I'll repeat it now: camouflaged jackets and khaki caps are just fine at Minsmere but when you're abroad if you must wear them at all make sure it's over a Hawaiian shirt or a pair of Mickey Mouse boxer shorts! Before you go out, take a look in the mirror and ask yourself: 'Do I look a bit like a terrorist?' If the answer is 'yes' (even a very little bit) – get changed immediately!

Having said all this, don't let me put you off the joys of foreign birding. I personally have survived many a trip without losing anything more than my dignity – and *I* even look a bit like Che Guevara!

A pretty sure way of avoiding most potential problems is to go with a group organized by one of the many specialist wildlife travel companies. It takes nearly all the pain out of it as it's the leader's job not only to make sure you're safe and comfortable but also to show you as many birds as possible. Can't be bad. (See Appendix, page 194.)

I really do recommend birding abroad. To me it has several attractions. There's the obvious fascination of travel and new places. Then there are the birds themselves, often exotic and beautiful and certainly different. There's also the challenge of recognizing species you'll never see in Britain and the satisfaction of getting to know some that you might. I have to admit this is my particular delight. No matter how wondrous the local specialities may be I am still drawn to the 'little brown job' that turns up as a rarity at home now and again.

I've *never* seen a Radde's Warbler in the UK. It's no great shame, it's a rare bird, and even if you try to twitch one it's so skulky you might easily miss it. In fact some years back I was staying on Scilly when a Radde's Warbler was supposedly resident for a week or more on the island of St Agnes. Every day somebody would see it, briefly but well enough to confirm it was still there. Three times I visited the island and sat by the little tangled field it was usually seen in. On the third day, I was there for over five hours. I never saw anything more than the flick of a tail on the other side of a bush that I eventually decided was 'probably' it. (The tail I mean, not the bush.) In fact looking back I reckon I was only trying to console myself. I certainly didn't tick it and, come to think of it, it could just as easiy have been a Wren!

Anyway, for years after that I was haunted by dreams of Radde's Warblers and whenever I heard that one had been reported somewhere I couldn't deny I felt a little twinge of envy and frustration. My dreams

A Radde's on a Thai rubbish dump.

continued until one day in Thailand, when they came true. I saw a Radde's Warbler. By the end of the day I'd seen several more, and by the end of the week I could recognize a Radde's at the flick of a tail, even if it *was* on the other side of a bush. As I said, I've *still* never seen one in this country. Most Octobers I hear reports of them, but I don't fret so much any more. I simply look forward to the day when I'll find one of my own – and not only will I recognize it immediately, it'll bring back happy memories of Thailand.

That I believe is one of the nice things about birding abroad – it sort of relaxes you, especially that little bit of twitcher in us all.

I'll give you another example. Something else I've not yet seen in Britain: a whole Pallas's Warbler. I've seen both ends, but never at the same time! It was on St Mary's (Scilly again) that I saw the tail. It was mid-October and I was ambling round with a friend trying to ignore the twitchers and find our own birds. At lunchtime we stopped at Holy Vale (a treelined valley justly famed for producing rare birds) and ate our sandwiches whilst gazing hopefully and, as it turned out, hopelessly into the foliage. By about four o'clock I was heading back along the road to the airport to catch the helicopter back to Cornwall where I was needed for filming early the next morning.

As we rounded a corner we were nearly run over by two birdwatchers on one bike. I didn't need to ask—I was told: 'Pallas's at Holy Vale'. I still had half an hour or so before the helicopter so we turned round and returned to Holy Vale where we arrived to find a gaggle of twenty or thirty birdwatchers sitting at the exact spot where we'd had our lunch. Had we missed it earlier or had it arrived during the afternoon? No time to consider that one, I had to see the bird quickly and get back to the airport. I'm not built for twitching, I'm only 5 foot 4 inches, so if I get stuck at the back I don't see very much. So, I crawled through a few pairs of legs and popped up in the front row. 'Where is it?' I gasped. 'There,' I was informed, 'in front of us.' Actually 'in front of us' was a wood full of trees that would easily have hidden a white rhino let alone a three-inch leaf-coloured warbler. Nobody dared take their binoculars off the bird so I had to find it myself. Eventually I did – just at the very moment it turned its back on us and dived deep into the shadows . . . never to return. Well at least not during the extra half hour I dared give myself, during which time I had to accept I'd missed the last helicopter. I resigned myself to the boat and I then literally ran the two or three miles back to the harbour with binoculars bashing my chest and telescope clobbering me in all sorts of sensitive places. ('Yomping' has nothing on a birdwatcher in a hurry and personally I'd send the Marines on a twitching course – that'd sort out the men from the princes.)

I arrived on the quayside as the *Scillonian* was actually pulling away and the gangplank was half up. A kindly mariner reduced the gap to a tantalizing couple of yards which, probably to everyone's disappointment, I safely lept. I was left hot, sweaty and puffed out and with the kind of moral dilemma that birdwatchers dread: could I tick half a Pallas's Warbler? At least I'd seen its yellow rump, which is a diagnostic feature, so it couldn't have been anything else, even if there'd been no one else there to tell me what I was looking for, I'd've recognized it myself anyway . . . wouldn't I? . . . . Probably. . . .

Anyway, I admit for nigh on five years there was literally half a tick, in pencil, on my check list. I got the other half at Portland. Again it was October, again I was filming for the BBC. I'd arranged with the very co-operative warden at the Bird Observatory that if anything good turned up they'd send a messenger up to our location and let me know so that I could get away and see whatever it was the next time we had a break. So, about ten o'clock one morning apparently a messenger duly arrived on the set bearing glad tidings. Unfortunately I was not visible to receive them. Ironically I was off birdwatching in the nearby quarries since I was not needed for an hour or two. The messenger, appropriately enough, left a message and went back to the Observatory, presumably to rejoin the rarity and its admirers. Eventually I re-appeared and the production assistant – who was not a birdwatcher of course – gave me the good news: 'They've caught a Crested Warbler.'

I was not immediately ecstatic. There is no such bird as a Crested Warbler! So what had it been? Well the day before there'd been a Yellow-browed Warbler in the area. I knew that, because I'd seen it. 'Do you mean Yellow-browed Warbler?' I ventured. 'Ah yes, *that'll* be it.' *He* seemed convinced, therefore so was I. 'Nice of them to come all this way to tell me that,' I thought, but since I'd seen a fair number of Yellow-broweds, even in the hand, and since I was now needed for filming, I didn't actually leap into my car and belt off for a quick twitch. Lunchtime came and I motored sedately down to the Observatory as was my daily wont. It seemed quiet. The warden was lounging on the balcony sipping a coffee with that air of satisfied relaxation only displayed by a birdwatcher who's just enjoyed a good bird. Yellow-broweds are good – but not *that* good. Did it really justify his looking so smug? 'Couldn't you get away then?' he asked, seeming puzzled at my nonchalance. 'Didn't seem worth it,' I replied. He seemed almost impressed: 'Oh . . . I suppose *you've* seen *lots* of Pallas's then.' I nearly wept. I mean I've heard of 'Chinese whispers' but how do you get 'Crested Warbler' from 'Pallas's Warbler' in one go? Mind you, come to think of it, it's a bit more plausible than 'Crested' from 'Yellow- browed'. 'It was great,' he assured me. 'We kept it as long as we could, but you never turned up so . . . we let it go.' 'Where?' 'There. In front of us.' My mind flashed back to Scilly. This time though the directions weren't quite so daunting. All I had to consider – 'in front of us' – was a short row of very small bushes and peeping out of one of them, visible even to the naked eye, was a little yellowy head. Up went my binoculars. There it was. A mass of stripes, over the crown, over the eye, I could even see one on the wing.

As if to say, 'OK you've seen me, can I carry on feeding now?' the little gem slipped backwards into the leaves whilst I accepted the offer of a coffee. For the remainder of the lunch break I sat on the balcony waiting for the bird to reappear and show the rest of itself. It never did. I walked over to the other side of the hedge, I walked all round it, I searched the Observatory garden and as much of the surrounding habitat as I had time to before I was due back on the set. In fact, nobody ever saw it again and no big twitch ensued. Nevertheless I'd seen enough, and that evening I added the other half of my tick.

The point of this ripping yarn? Well, I'm still waiting to see the complete bird in Britain and every autumn there's plenty reported but it never really bothers me much, not since a magical morning in the botanical gardens at Godaveri in Nepal when I stood beneath a single tree that was alive with flickering, fluttering little birds, at least fifty of them, every one a Pallas's Warbler – both ends at once.

Two Pallas's Warblers . . . or one very long one?

A Final Thought ...

From Birmingham to Bangkok, from Kent to Kathmandhu, wherever you are birdwatching the principles and techniques are the same, and so are the problems, the challenges and the joys.

It quite simply is a wonderful way to spend your time. If you're already a birdwatcher, or you're thinking of getting into it please do me a favour – or rather do yourself a favour – *never give it up.*

Appendix

How to become the complete birdwatcher . . . as quickly as possible.

Periodicals you simply must get . . .

British Birds

The monthly magazine. It does have some fairly scientific papers and elaborate articles on identification but it is by no means difficult or abstruse. Lots of great photos and illustrations. To quote myself: 'You can't call yourself a real birdwatcher until you're a *British Birds* reader' – and nobody paid me to say that!

For *free* sample copy: Mrs Erika Sharrock, Fountains, Park Lane, Blunham, Bedford MK44 3NJ.

Bird Watching Magazine
Also monthly and now available from all good newsagents, so I needn't
give an address.

Also well worth getting even if you can't read Dutch (a lot of it's in
English anyway) *Dutch Birding*. Address: Dutch Birding, Postbus 5611,
1007 AP Amsterdam, Holland.

Societies you must join . . .

The RSPB (Royal Society for the Protection of Birds). Any birdwatcher
who is not a member ought to have their binoculars confiscated! And for
youngsters the YOC (Young Ornithologists Club). Both great value for
membership money with superb quarterly magazines *Birds* and *Bird Life*.
Address for both: The Lodge, Sandy, Beds, SE19 2DL. Tel: 0767 80551.

And . . . your local Bird Club or Naturalists Trust. Nearly every region
in the country has one, possibly under a county heading, eg the Dorset
Bird Club, or a group of counties – e.g., The West Midland Bird Club,
Addresses are listed in the *Birdwatchers Year Book* which is published
annually by Buckingham Press. This book is *so* useful I'm putting it at the
top of the . . .

Essential Books

First . . . where to buy them. Remember few shops have a decent
selection so ask for catalogues and mail order from The *British Birds*
Book Shop list published in the magazine, or The Natural History Book
Service, 2 Wills Road, Totnes, Devon TQ9 5XN. Tel: 0803 865913.

For general information and addresses of birdclubs, societies, bird
observatories, reserves and so on . . . as I said . . . you must get a current
copy of *The Birdwatchers Year Book*.

For even more detail on Bird Observatories
Bird Observatories in Britain and Ireland (Poyser)

And on RSPB Reserves
RSPB Nature Reserves (RSPB)

Where to watch Birds?
The New Where to Watch Birds (John Gooders, Deutsch)
Birdwatching in Britain – a site by site guide (Nigel Redman and Simon
Harrap, Helm)

Identification

Field guides . . . as used by the country's top birdwatchers!

Field Guides for use in Britain

The Shell Guide to the Birds of Britain and Ireland by Ferguson-Lees, Willis & Sharrock

A Field Guide to the Birds of Britain and Europe by Peterson, Mountfort & Hollom

The Birds of Britain and Europe with North Africa and the Middle East by Heinzel, Fitter & Parslow

Birds of Britain and Europe by Bruun, Delin, Svensson, Singer & Zetterström

Field Guide to the Birds of Britain and Ireland by Gooders & Harris

The RSPB Book of British Birds by Holden, Sharrock & Burn

Field Guides for use in Europe

A Field Guide to the Birds of Britain and Europe by Peterson, Mountfort & Hollom

Birds of Britain and Europe by Bruun, Delin, Svensson, Singer & Zetterström

Birds of the Mediterranean and Alps by Lars Jonsson

The Birds of Britain and Europe with North Africa and the Middle East by Heinzel, Fitter & Parslow

The Shell Guide to the Birds of Britain and Ireland by Ferguson-Lees, Willis & Sharrock

Field Guides for use in North Africa and the Middle East

The Birds of Britain and Europe with North Africa and the Middle East by Heinzel, Fitter & Parslow

Birds of Britain and Europe by Bruun, Delin, Svensson, Singer & Zetterström

A Field Guide to the Birds of Britain and Europe by Peterson, Mountfort & Hollom

The Shell Guide to the Birds of Britain and Ireland by Ferguson-Lees, Willis & Sharrock

Birds of Britain and Europe by Bruun, Delin, Svensson, Singer & Zetterström (Country Life Books) 2nd edn 1986.

And *Identification Guides* on groups of birds

Seabirds: *An Identification Guide* by Peter Harrison (Christopher Helm)

Shorebirds: *An Identification Guide* by Hayman, Marchant and Prater (Christopher Helm)

Birds of Prey of Britain and Europe by Benny Gensbol (Collins)

Flight Identification of European Raptors by Porter, Willis, Christensen and Nielsen, (Poyser)

Gulls – A Guide to Identification by P.J. Grant (Poyser)

Wildfowl: An identification guide by Steve Madge and Hilary Burn (Christopher Helm)

Bird Photography: *A Field Guide to Photographing Birds* by Dr Mike Hill and Gordon Langsbury (Collins)

Drawing Birds: *Drawing Birds* by John Busby (RSPB)

And more birdwatchers choices . . . from *British Birds* Surveys.

Top 18 binoculars for 1985

Zeiss West Dialyt 10×40B
Leitz Trinovid 10×40B
Zeiss Jena Jenoptem 10×50
Optolyth Alpin 10×50
Optolyth Alpin 10×40
Swift Audubon 8.5×44
Leitz Trinovid 8×40B
Habicht Diana 10×40
Zeiss Jena Notarem 10×40B

Zeiss Jena Jenoptem 8×30
Mirador 10×40
Optolyth Alpin 8×40
Zeiss Jena Dekarem 10×50
Swift Osprey 7.5×42
Swift Trilyte 10×40B
Swift Newport 10×50
Pentax 8×40
Ross Stepruva 9×35

Top 18 telescopes for 1985

Optolyth 30×75GA
Bushnell Spacemaster ×60 wce
Kowa TS-1/TS-2 ×60 wce
Bushnell/Bausch & Lomb Discoverer 15-60×60
Optolyth 30×80GA
Hertel & Reuss Televari 25-60×60
Swarovski Habicht 30×75
Optolyth 22-60×70GA
Mirador ×60 wce
Opticron High resolution ×60 wce
Questar (mirrorlens) wce
Swift Telemaster 15-60×60
Opticron Piccolo ×60 wce
Optolyth 22×60GA
Nickel Supra 15-60×60
Schmidt & Bender 15-60×60
Optima ×60 wce
Greenkat ×60 wce

Weather Proof Jackets (manufacturers)

Helly Hansen
Rohan
Functional
Mountain Equipment
Greenfell
Barbour
Tiklas
Britton
Walkabout
Fjällräven
Ultimate
Berghaus
Greenspot
Mascot

Bradsport
Damart/Goredale
Macbean
Husky
Keeperware
Sprayway
Marks & Spencer
Peter Storm
Nevissport
Henri-Lloyd
North Cape
Thornproof
Walrus
Belstaff

Bird Holiday Tour Companies

Field Studies Council
Birding
Sunbird
Caledonian Wildlife
Tom Gullick
Birdquest
Swan Hellenic
Twickers World
Cygnus Wildlife
Ornitholidays
Branta Travel
IBIS Tours
RSPB Holidays
Cox & Kings
Peregrine Holidays
Chris L. Slade

I'd like to thank *British Birds* for making these survey results available and indeed for doing the surveys in the first place; but I must stress most strongly that such lists are likely to go out of date pretty rapidly as new products appear and old ones disappear. I certainly haven't published prices, because they're bound to have gone up already!

So I apologise most heartily to any producers of good stuff that have been left out and please don't necessarily assume that anything not on the list must be below standard. Not at all – it just might be the new improved model we've all been waiting for!

The original, more detailed, versions are available from *British Birds* at a small price.

Twitching

For access to *the* hot line on up to the minute bird news join The Bird Information Service (BIS), Appletree Cottage, Marshside, Brancaster, King's Lynn, Norfolk PE31 8AD. Tel: 0485 210349 (for membership details *not* bird news). You'll also get a rather neat little magazine that will give you all sorts of vicarious excitement or make you green with envy depending on your disposition. Personally, I love reading it – all the thrills with none of the discomfort.

Birding Abroad

For all the 'gen', send a 50p postal order for a catalogue to Steve Whitehouse The Foreign Birdwatching and Reports Service, 5 Stanway Close, Blackpole, Worcester WR4 9XL or phone (0905) 54541.

Index